Reimagining Education @ REVA

Reimagining Education
@
REVA

Dr. P. Shyama Raju

REVA UNIVERSITY
Bengaluru, India

in association with

New Century Publications
New Delhi, India

New Century Publications
4800 / 24, Bharat Ram Road,
Ansari Road, Daryaganj,
New Delhi - 110 002 (India)

Tel.: 011-2324 7798, 4358 7398, 4101 7798

E-mail: info@newcenturypublications.com

www.newcenturypublications.com

Editorial Office:
4832/24, Ansari Road, Daryaganj,
New Delhi – 110 002

Tel.: 011-4356 0919

First Published: **2020**

ISBN: **978-81-7708-510-5**

Published by New Century Publications and printed at Milan Enterprises, New Delhi.

Designs: Patch Creative Unit, New Delhi.

PRINTED IN INDIA

*For all edupreneurs who have ventured into education
and where the learning begins
all over again*

*For my children and grandchildren whose immense
support in my life has translated my dreams into reality*

About the Book

The objective of publishing this dossier is to ensure that we have a guideline in place as a part of our Post-COVID readiness for the University to function. The guideline has been prepared bearing in mind the fact that if the situations that we live in grow adverse or remain unviable, REVA is future-ready and prepared to face any challenge.

Hence, the book that started as a dossier, also carries an insight into the COVID time challenges that REVA University faced undauntingly. The REVA team worked almost magically, covering the syllabus, extended remote support, with consistent and planned remote instruction, online support for counselling and also online assessments and evaluation leading to results being released timely. The book traverses through the last few months chronicling each stage of the University during these difficult times, in the form of captured images, anecdotes, student testimonials and also detailed notes for deeper understanding of the process in most sections.

Placement, skill development, employment engagement programmes, webinars, international conferences, training and support for faculty, guest talks were all part of this tapestry of revolutionary education and together REVA Reimagined Education!

While guidelines are being laid by many agencies including the UN for reopening of educational institutions, care and forethought is required independently by each of us and therefore I felt the need to bring out a compiled book for our benefit, which perhaps can be a guide for others too.

About the Author

Nurturing the change-makers of tomorrow is a big responsibility, and this is exactly what Dr. P. Shyama Raju has executed with seamless perfection. An indefatigable champion of higher education in India, this determined leader is a known figure in the country. He is a top educationist who is deeply involved in the process of providing the best education and nurturing the healthiest environment for the exchange of this scale. His clear vision of how learning should be imparted has brought a paradigm shift in the education sector.

Dr. Raju's success story started with being an entrepreneur. After acquiring a degree in Commerce from SGS Arts College, Tirupati, he established DivyaSree Developers Pvt. Ltd, a Real Estate Development Company that has successfully spearheaded several construction spectacles across the country. In the last 4 decades of its existence, the Group has carved a niche for itself by triumphantly shaping several IT parks, residential developments, infrastructure projects, and built-to-suit campuses. Orchestrating technical expertise, global best practices, and project management skills, DivyaSree Developers has consistently built benchmarks and created valuable assets.

The incredible success of DivyaSree was quickly followed up with the establishment of Rukmini Educational Charitable Trust, an organization that is involved in the pursuit of providing aid to the growing need for quality education and philanthropic quests for the environment and general awareness. Dr. Shyama Raju also founded the REVA Group of Educational Institutions under Rukmini Educational Charitable Trust which reinstated REVA in its present form in 2004. Today, REVA University is a torchbearer in the field of higher learning, moving steadily up the rankings in excellence.

Raising education standards countrywide, Dr. Raju is a motivational leader who inspires upright practices and constantly monitors and evaluates the quality of education being *meted* out to the students. He is celebrated for his resilient focus on creating a better India by encouraging quality education and research, relevant to social needs. An ardent philanthropist, Dr. P. Shyama Raju has been personally involved in all CSR and University Outreach activities of the University. Under his aegis, the University made waves in the country as he introduced Jagruti, a social outreach campaign from REVA that witnessed three phases: Jagruti towards electoral awareness which made news during the last elections of the country, educating youth about their electoral rights, Jagruti towards global warming, wherein he spearheaded a digital campaign towards raising global awareness in youth and Jagruti towards COVID-19 which is now making every attempt in the current scenario to raise a positive awareness in all realms of the world.

The strong-minded leader ensures talent retention at REVA by offering complete academic freedom to every single member of the faculty. He has beefed up a team of highly illustrious academicians who work in perfect sync to his vision. He has amplified success by creating a decorous environment for learning.

In acknowledgement of his profound efforts made in the education sector, he has been conferred with many prestigious Awards. He was awarded an Honorary Doctorate (Honoris Causa) by the prestigious Visvesvaraya Technological University, Belagavi in 2015 for his outstanding contribution to Higher Education and Learning.

He was presented with the Sir M. Visvesvaraya Shiromani Award for being a Visionary Educationist in 2016, followed by the high-status Karnataka Rajyotsava Award 2017 by the Karnataka State Government. He was also recognized as Global Asian of the year 2017 and Most Exemplary Leader in Internationalization of Indian Education Forum, 2018 in the Parliament House, UK. He graced the cover of Forbes India March 2019 edition as one of the top Global Leaders of the Country.

In future, this impassioned leader aspires to focus on higher realms of education and spearhead REVA to be a research and innovation seeking University.

Contents

Preface

The objective behind publishing this dossier is to ensure that we have a guideline in place as a part of our Post COVID readiness for the University to function. The guideline is prepared bearing in mind the fact that if the situations that we live in grow adverse or remain unviable, REVA is future-ready and prepared to face any challenge. Hence, the book that started as a dossier, also carries an insight into the COVID time challenges that REVA University faced undauntingly. The REVA team worked almost magically, covering the syllabus, extended remote support, with consistent and planned remote instruction, online support for counselling and also online assessments and evaluation leading to results being released timely.

The book traverses through the last few months chronicling each stage of the University during these difficult times, in the form of captured images, anecdotes, student testimonials and also detailed notes for deeper understanding of the process in most sections. Placement, skill development, employment engagement programs, webinars, international conferences, training and support for faculty, guest talks all of it were a part of this tapestry of Revolutionary education and together REVA Reimagined Education! The book serves more as a ready reckoner chronicling the best practices of REVA for any other young University to emulate.

From me to you...

As we embark on a new journey post COVID, let me at the outset thank teachers, parents and all stakeholders for all the support extended to our students and for the courage that all have exhibited in these times. Reopening Education Institutions post COVID will be one of the greatest challenges of the times, considering the fact that as per UNESCO estimates, more than 155 crore students are impacted due to the pandemic outbreak. The world was unprepared for this as we continued to live in our glassed existence unaware of what was in store for us. COVID warning and its widespread shadow impacted educational institutions the most as large number of students gather in campuses and use all the facilities within the ecosystem. We have to continue forward and work together and hence we need to ensure that we have proper directives in place.

While guidelines are being laid by many agencies including the UN for reopening of Educational Institutions, care and forethought is required independently by each of us and therefore I felt we need to bring together a compiled book for our benefit, which perhaps can be a guide for younger Universities to follow.

The youth and their education cannot be impacted for long as their wellbeing and their future will be jeopardised. At the same time, health and hygiene services are of utmost importance for each campus to drastically reduce the risk of health to the youth. Balancing physical health with nutrition and care and also at the same time ensuring there is mental and psychosocial well-being is the greatest challenge. The guidelines as penned for REVA captures our ecosystem needs and has been designed to make it flexible and open ended. I am sure there will unanticipated situations and unforeseen contingencies that we will all have to be ready for.

The book looks at the following key priorities:

- Readiness of REVA in Retrospect,
- Reset: Campus Opening Plan, and
- Recovery Strategies for REVA: The New Normal.

Let us make a conscientious effort to ensure that we add on to this repertoire that we have built and share this as a part of our learning experience and a guide for all those who we can support during these times. The purpose of this book is to ensure that we have clear and actionable guidance for safe operations during these days and arresting the spread of the virus apart from maintaining a safe University campus. Being independent, Private State Universities we will have to prepare our own pandemic roadmaps, while adhering to the guidelines set by the Government and bearing in mind all safety, health and guidance measures related to the virus.

Bengaluru
July 2020

Dr. P. Shyama Raju
Chancellor

1

Readiness of REVA in Retrospect

1.1 Re-Shaping the Future

Education is a systematic process of disseminating knowledge to the target audience. This process has to be revisited with a new perspective keeping the current scenario and future into consideration. Usually, education is often understood as a process that takes place in formal settings but it is not true. Education can take place either in a formal or an informal setting. Education today is a process that aims at enhancing knowledge, skills, attitude, behavior, personality, perceptions, values, beliefs and ability to assess. Education should not be considered as a tool to settle down in life with a good job, but it should aim at preparing each one of us to lead a life that is satisfying and gratifying to us. Maturity in our thoughts, views, and actions is important and education should focus on these aspects. Education according to me is an experience which helps to be better individuals. It should also empower us to develop a positive understanding of the world around us.

Each one of us may have different expectation and experience that we might get through the process of education, but most of all education should help us to progress positively in the desired directions.

Indian culture and tradition teaches us not only the right value systems, principles, values, ethics but also imbibes in us disciplines which is very important for any individual. Indian mythology has also educated us with strong educative values, whether it is our Vedas, Upanishads, Bhagavad-Gita, Ramayana or Mahabharata. All of these has helped us to relate history to the present context to learn and educate ourselves.It could be Durga through whom we have learnt lessons of power, authority and leadership or it could be the last battle of Mahabharata which involved lessons of strategic planning. Even today we can relate, correlate and learn many lessons from every character, situation or scenario.

When I say this that situation or scenario can help us learn many things, I would like to relate this with the present prevailing situation of COVID-19 that has made us or forced us to rethink and also understand the actual meaning of uncertainty. Uncertainty is a word that can be understood in simple words as something that we are not sure of, like what is happening and what may happen. As we understand the actual meaning of uncertainty during this dreadful pandemic that has shaken the whole world, affected the world economy, all sectors of the economy be it Politics, Government, Banking Sector, Real Estate, Transportation, Tourism, Hotel, Healthcare, IT sector. Even the education sector has been affected by the prevailing pandemic and uncertainty persists because of the same. Being an educationist I ventured into education 15 years back, made a modest beginning and started first the REVA Group of Educational Institutions and over the period of time due to contribution of all my stakeholders that is management, staff both teaching and non-teaching, parents, statutory and governing bodies, state government and most importantly because of the achievements and progress made by our students and alumni today REVA is a brand in the educational spectrum where we have been identified as REVA University.

Driven by a strong vision and mission we stay committed to our stakeholder's society at large in providing education that would meet the global standards, with state-of-the-art infrastructure facility which makes teaching-learning process conducive.

REVA is a Temple of Learning, wherein we believe in the motto 'Knowledge is Power' and when I say knowledge is power it means that we emphasize on the fact that knowledge should empower us to explore, experience and excel with new thoughts, ideas and views that can be truly translated into reality. Organization cannot be built with bricks, stones, iron and cement, organizations are built with trust, faith and worthy committed people. Ups and downs are quite natural in any sector and with my immense experience in the field of business, I have faced many challenges personally and professionally which has enabled me to experience learn and understand as to how to handle the situation.

Of course COVID-19 pandemic has disturbed the academic process and left each one of us clueless as to what should be done in a situation like this. In the current scenario we have not only understood the meaning of uncertainty but we have also understood the importance of foreseeing the future. I would define change as something that disturbs the normal pattern of work. Change always initially will be strongly resisted because nobody will be interested in accepting new changes. Therefore, resistance to change is usually the first obstacle that we face in the process of change but nevertheless, change is a must and it is inevitable. Even though it takes time for each one of us to understand the intensity of the prevailing situation, let us not close our eyes nor block our mind and become an hurdle in the process of change.

Whenever we talk about change, we have also heard about resistance to change, but let me tell you that resistance is temporary and acceptance is going to be permanent. To bring in change, studying and analyzing the present scenario is important and along with that foreseeing the future is also equally important. Any change brought in to the system without anticipating the future consequences would indeed fail and the reason is because we were not able to understand the future needs and requirements.

Change should be planned systematically and must be in a phased manner. Changes that will be implemented should be critically examined in terms of pros and cons. Any change that will be brought into the system, at least 40-50% of the changes that is introduced, will become permanent. Therefore, careful planning and implementation is must.

Whenever there is an emergency we immediately get into the crisis management mode, nothing wrong at that point of time handling the crisis and resolving becomes our priority. But any solutions that you record during a crisis is just a temporary solution that may give us a soothing effect for a shorter duration of time.

Today, all universities, educational institutions, schools, pre-schools are all doing the same that is to stay connected with their students and to continue the teaching learning process. Each one of them have adopted their own ways and approaches and tried to give their best to the student community, which needs to be highly appreciated. But the question that arises before each one of us is the effectiveness of the process. Ultimately, we should be able to reach out to our target audience effectively. In these changing times when health and safety plays a important role the education we impart should also emphasize on the same.

Any change introduced in a uncertain situation like COVID-19 specially with respect to education will surely bring in lots of questions from the stakeholders.

Impact of Change on Stakeholders

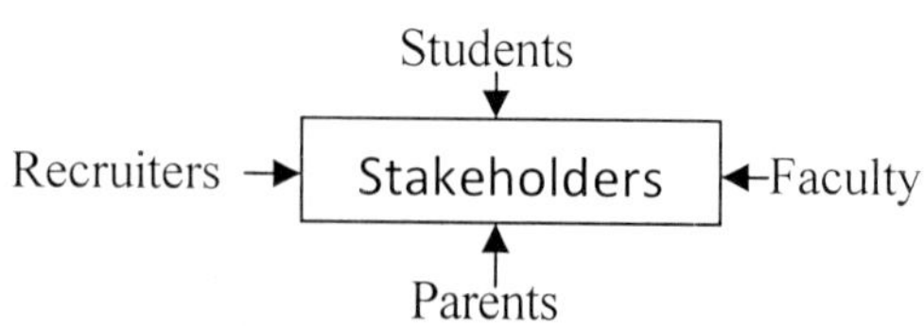

Students: The current pandemic has absolutely disturbed the students and their dreams, it has created anxiety in them, they are worried about their academics and career, concerned about campus safety, confused about future, fear of failure, change and inability to adapt to technology.

Faculty: Faculty form a very integral part of the teaching-learning process playing the role of a facilitator and used to conventional mode of teaching and learning. Today they are expected to adapt themselves to a new work culture, changes in the work culture, changes in the organization, adapting technology in teaching and learning and fear of loss of job.

Recruiters: Recruiters are worried about the onboarding of the students who have been hired by them through campus selections and their preparedness to join the organization in this situation. The recruiters are also concerned that due to the pandemic the newly hired students will have to be given work from home option, where they may not be in a position to familiarize, orient and give them a thorough induction which may not be possible by them due to the current COVID-19 situation.

Parents: Today we come across cases where most of them have a single child and they are more concerned for their child. Be it a single child or even more that, as a parent, their main concern is health and safety of the child. They are also concerned about the academics, career and future of their wards and most importantly during this situation indeed more parental care and support is required.

So change has impacted each one of us. Stakeholders have their own reasons to be worried, but there I would like to emphasise that it is not the time to panic or worry but rather it is a time to diligently plan and act.

As a family head of REVA University despite being a senior citizen I believed that if I have to answer all my stakeholders then it is important for me to lead from front and take steps that would help all the stakeholders. There is need for us to re-think, re-define our processes and also re-imagine the future of education. Reforms in education is very much needed and quite often this sector is forgotten. I would rather say a thorough introspection is needed to understand the future needs and requirements. This understanding will enable us to plan, prepare and implement the process effectively. Change has to be experimented and evaluated critically. Society has faced such uncertain situations in the past and let me tell you that there is no one formula or solution that suits all problems. Acting as per the situation is important. COVID-19 is just few months old in India. There is no need to react or panic to the situation in a very big way but instead of reacting; acting to the situation appropriately is a wise thought. Do not aim at changing the system of education but instead aim at changing your mindset and re-look into the process and I am sure you will be able to adapt and adjust to the new normal and in course of time you will get accustomed to the new normal that will enable you to be better individuals personally and professionally. In this context, is documented in the next few sections of the book, my takeaways at REVA in these times.

1.2 The Advent of COVID-19

Keeping in mind the COVID-19 situation, which came unannounced and unprecedented in history; at REVA we were quick to react to the situation and both the teaching staff and students adapted themselves to the new situation. It was unanimously decided to ensure that all schools move to remote instruction second week of March, 2020 itself. Both faculty and students in this time of the year are generally busy with covering their scheduled portions, assignments and also extra classes. COVID impacted the academic rigour of the program. The team was quick and ready with alternate measures of learning and within no time REVA went ahead and implemented online teaching and support. In its perspective plan for the University, REVA had always been a forerunner in digitalizing the campus as depicted in Figure 1.1.

Figure 1.1: Digital REVA

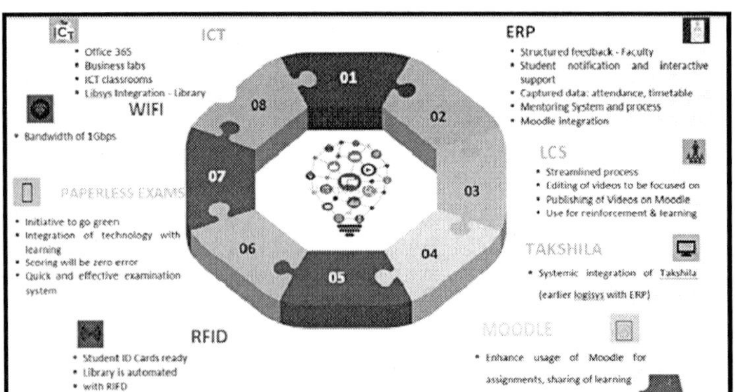

REVA had a LCS system in campus, where important lectures are captured and beamed to students. Faculty were already in the practice of using this facility for students for their recap sessions. The ERP was always used to populate all course handouts, ppts of topics and notes to students. LMS and moodle was even otherwise in use for assignment submission. Whatsapp notes were used in specific groups for students during these times as well so as to reach out to remote area students.

For regular assessments, quizzes were given by faculty on Moodle. More than anything the faculty were available online for student related queries. These are the advantages of being a technology driven University.

Directors of Schools and Mentors were in constant touch with the parent community and kept sending them mailers about the developments at REVA. The faculty who were mentors continued mentoring students, personally supervising students and completely immersed in remote instruction. MS Teams was used to the maximum to reach out to students and also support them in all aspects. A chronological capture of the events follows for a quicker understanding of how prepared REVA was to face the new situation (Figure 1.2).

Figure 1.2: Tracking Chronologically the COVID Times

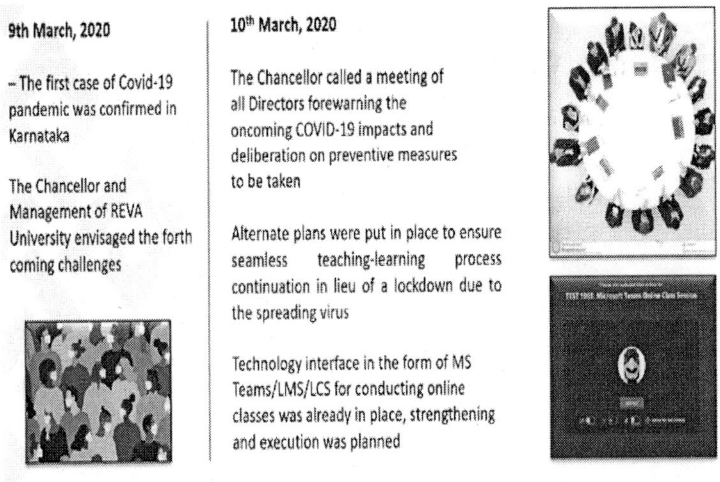

12th March, 2020:

All Directors attended series of training sessions for MS Teams to strengthen academic governance and online meetings

12th March, 2020

onwards faculty were trained on use of MS Teams

In sequence....

13th March, 2020:

Govt. of Karnataka (ED 107 UNE 2020 Dt. 13/03/2020) sent a circular ordering closing of University Activities from **14/03/2020 to 29/03/2020**

16th March, 2020 :

Classes online started for all schools Government of India- declared the first lockdown: **25th March-14th April 2020**

1.3 Continuing Digital Support

The prevalent situation in the world made me promptly work on the required IT support and ensuring that there were enough refresher courses conducted for faculty apart from training from the Microsoft team to ensure that there was adequate support given to the teaching fraternity.

What was priority was ensuring that the campus was ready for quick adaptation to the situation and also ensuring that teaching does not get affected in any form.

At the same time, it was important that the core office kept communication going with all stakeholders and therefore mailers were sent to staff, students and to parents (Figure 1.3) keeping them dated of the happenings and the campus readiness.

Figure 1.3: Emailer for Campus Readiness (Students)

REVA UNIVERSITY
Bengaluru, India

Our Commitment

“

Dear REVAite,

Greetings to you and pray that you are all safe and healthy apart from strictly observing social distancing!

I am happy that your faculty at REVA has been supporting you through remote teaching and also giving you assignments and assessments. Team REVA is proud that we were able to rise to the demands of the situation, ensure our hostellers and all of you are safe. For those of you who have been placed by REVA career development centre, please be assured that your transition from the campus to the corporate will be taken care of. REVA counsellors have also been conducting online emotional counselling for students. Do not hesitate to talk to them if need be. Keeping the students engaged and ensuring that your learning is not affected at any cost was our major focus and I am happy to share with you that we have been successful at this.

At this moment, I am also concerned about those of our students who are housed in remote parts of the country and with limited access to technology. We would like to assure you that all our teachers are ready to support you through various platforms like phone calls, SMS, WhatsApp and emails and will be more than happy to support. We are also in the process of closing our decision on alternate methods of assessment and will communicate soon with you in this regard. I want you to reach out to your faculty for all learning support as and when required.

I will personally moniter this exercise with all Directors and also put in place a feedback system from each student. In the meantime, please write to info@reva.edu.in for swift responses and support.

”

I would also like to add with pride that:

- REVA is ready for an extension of lockdown or contingency and will support students in their progress
- We are ready to commence the semester in time without affecting the quality and with commitment to carry forward all classes
- All online payments are encouraged and students need not go to banks for any payment
- Assessments will be online and we will ensure timely release of results
- Admission process is on and students have been taking up REVA CET online
- Our admission counsellors have been personally counselling students using video calls, WhatsApp calls and other modes of communication
- Our campus is safe and all security measures are amplified

I look forward to your understanding and compassion during these times so as to reaffirm the trust of all of you in our **Temple of Learning**

Keep well! Stay safe!

Dr P Shyama Raju
Chancellor
REVA University

Figure 1.3: Emailer to Parents

REVA UNIVERSITY

Bengaluru, India

Our Commitment

“

Dear parent,

Greetings to you and pray that you are all safe and healthy apart from strictly observing social distancing!

I am sure you are aware that the REVA team and faculty have been supporting our students through online teaching and also giving them assignments and assessments. We at REVA are proud that we were able to rise to the demands of the situation, ensure our hostellers and all other students are safe. Our Placement Team will ensure that students whose placements are done through REVA career development centre are smoothly transitioned to their workplace. REVA counsellors have also been conducting online emotional counselling for students during these times. Keeping the students engaged and ensuring that their learning is not affected at any cost, was our major focus and I am happy to share with you that we have been successful in this and most of the modules of the students have been completed as per schedule.

At this moment, I am also concerned about those of our students who are housed in remote parts of the country and with limited access to technology. We would like to assure you that all our teachers are ready to support our students through various platforms like phone calls, SMS, WhatsApp, emails and will be more than happy to do so. We are also in the process of closing our decision on alternate methods of assessment and will communicate soon with you in this regard. Please encourage your child to reach out to their faculty for all learning support and our teachers will be there to support them with clarification or doubts.

I will personally monitor this exercise with all Directors and also put in place a feedback system from each student while students can write to us on info@reva.edu.in so as to ensure that support is extended swiftly.

”

I would also like to add with pride that:

- REVA is ready for an extension of lockdown or contingency and will support students in their progress
- We are ready to commence the semester in time without affecting the quality and with commitment to carry forward all classes
- All online payments are encouraged and students need not go to banks for any payment
- Assessments will be online and we will ensure timely release of results
- Admission process is functional and students have been taking up REVA CET online
- Our admission counsellors have been personally counselling students using video calls, WhatsApp calls and other modes of communication
- Virtual tours can be arranged for students on request to the Admission office
- Our campus is safe and all security measures are beefed up

I look forward to your understanding and compassion during these times so as to reaffirm the trust of all of you in our **Temple of Learning**

Keep well! Stay safe!

Dr P Shyama Raju
Chancellor
REVA University

At the same time, evacuating the student residents from the campus was prime and hostellers were given adequate notice and assurance that they would be safe at their homes. Students who needed support to reach their destination were spoken to and parents were well connected with so that even the international students reached their destinations safely (Figure 1.4).

Figure 1.4: Communique with International Students

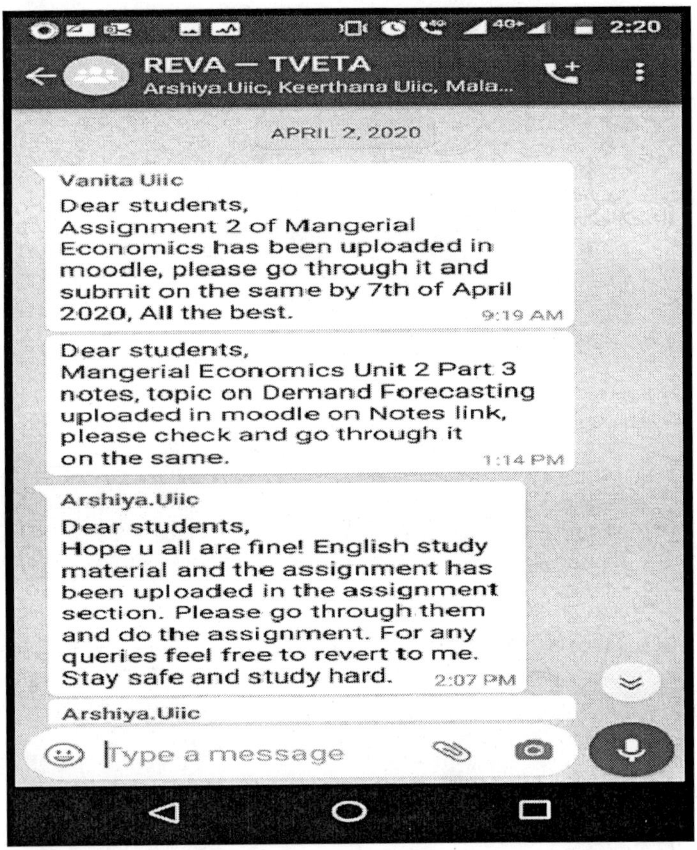

Figure 1.4: Communique with International Students

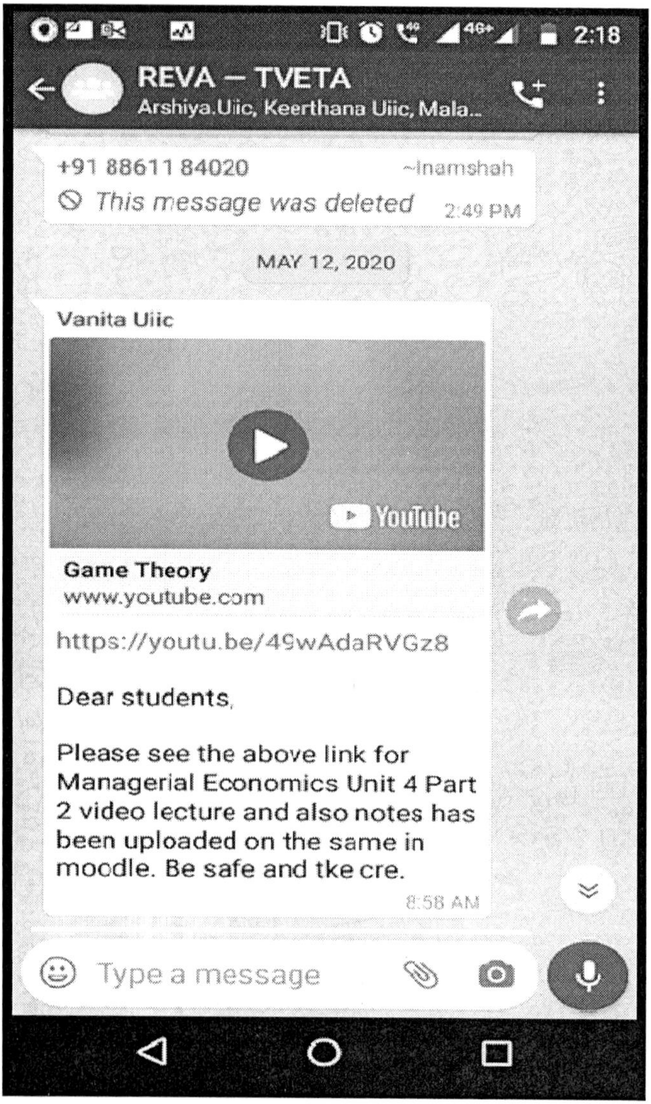

Figure 1.4: Communique with International Students

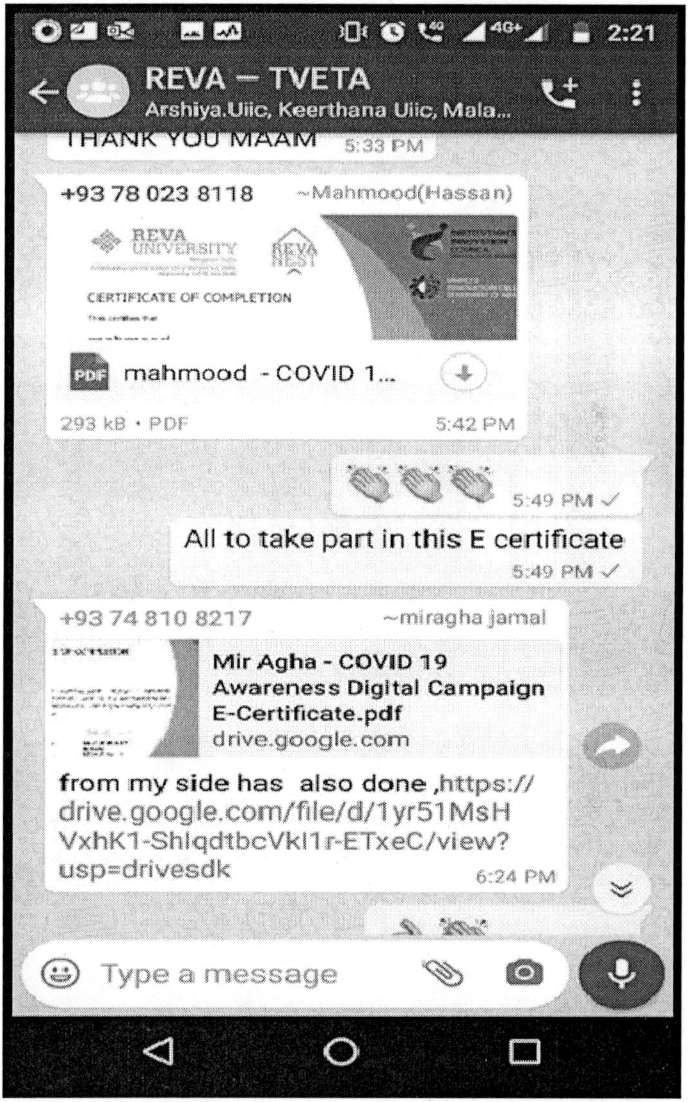

Figure 1.4: Communique with International Students

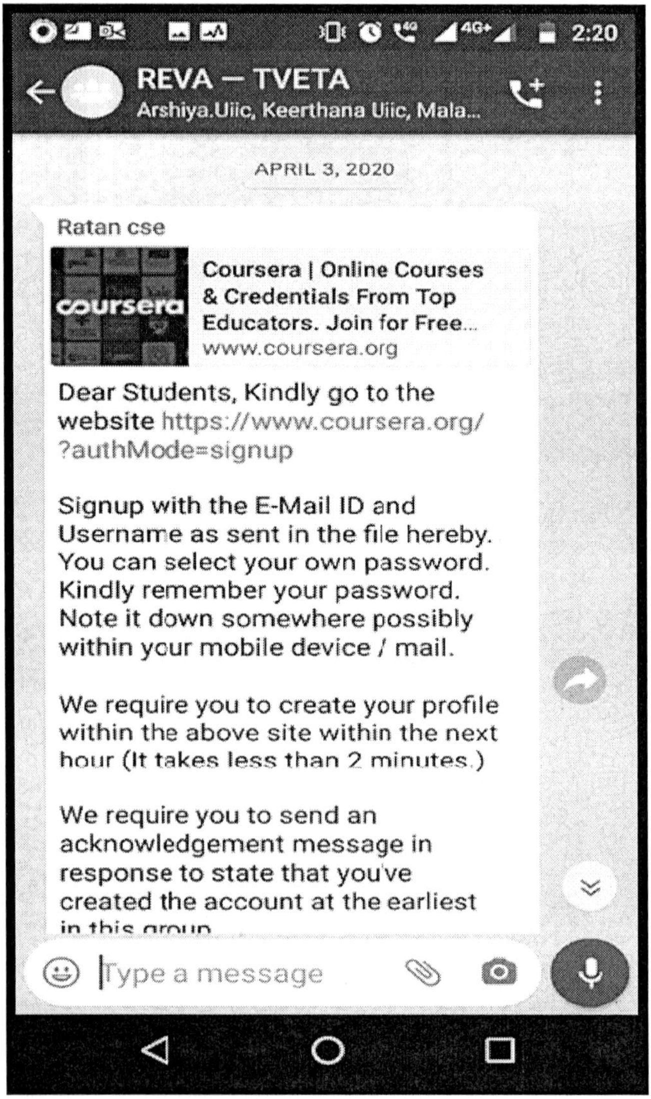

Classes for international students was also conducted online. These classes were scheduled in such a manner that it was suitable as per timings in their countries (Figure 1.5).

Figure 1.5: Online Classes for International Students

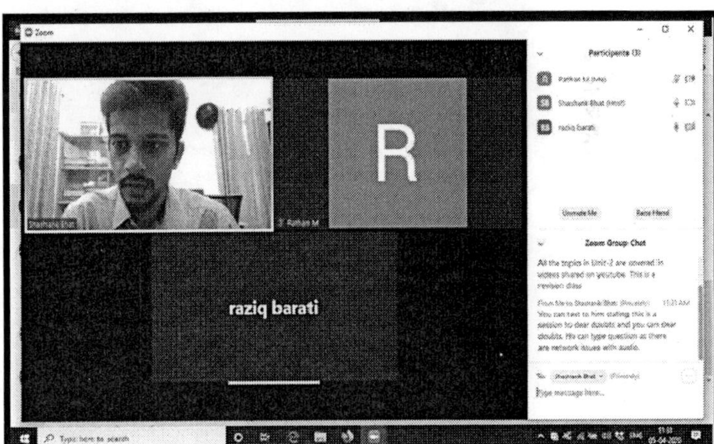

1.4 Vantage Point @ REVA

REVA always believed in going Digital and the last five year efforts were in ensuring that the perspective plan set for the University is met with in all aspects. Hence, these times of COVID did not hamper the teaching-learning system at REVA. Online classes continued to be an integral part of the REVA academic program and the B School had many programs run as ancillary programs too to support the students in all aspects and enrich their skills.

In accordance with this objective in mind, Coursera for Campus had already been initiated and implemented by REVA University for the academic year 2020-2021. In its first phase and keeping COVID conditions in mind, more than 5000 free Coursera for Campus licenses were given to students and focus was on skill development courses and courses that would add value to the outgoing student profile. With Coursera in Campus, the objective is to enable our University to offer high quality, job-relevant, online learning to students and faculty. REVA being one of the youngest Multi-Disciplinary Universities in India, the vision is to ensure learners are benefitted from these courses.

Apart from this, the Career Development Centre ensured that online training in personality development and all course based employability enhancement programs were run online. The University also offers in normal times a blended mode of learning as core courses are offered offline and most of the electives, employability enhancement programmes, skill development courses and life skills development courses were offered online.

1.4.1 Teaching Learning Support: During COVID-19 for instance, every single class was taken up starting March, 2020 and that which continued for the PG classes. Listing them categorically is shown on next page:

1. Students not only attended lecture hours but were given virtual demo sessions, practical class sessions and case studies.

2. Project support and assignments and IA was conducted in a timely manner.
3. Student feedback and parent feedback was taken occasionally and several academic governance sessions, mentoring sessions were taken up online by the University.
4. Staff engaged in meetings and also the University went ahead with international conferences as scheduled, hackathons and also webinars and guest talks from international faculty.
5. Coursera for Campus was given to students free of cost so that skill development sessions for the senior classes could go on without any disturbance in their placement schedules.
6. The Career Development Centre took it upon themselves to ensure that they arranged virtual meetings and placements with the industry continued.
7. Online examination has been planned in a timely phase and since REVA follows a paperless exam mode, it was easier for students to adapt themselves to the online assessments plan.
8. Lecture Capturing system was used to the maximum and students could retrieve these lectures as and when they required for revision.
9. Students from rural areas also benefitted from this as WhatsApp and other platforms were also used to support these students.
10. The campus being a wifi campus and with functional residential staff, the staff did not hesitate to support students academically at any point of time.

With technology and integration of technology remaining prime for the University, REVA is digital right from ERP usage to Lecture Capturing systems to ICT support in all lecture halls, to tab based assessment, to online assessments to usage of Office 365 and MS Teams for seamless integration of technology in learning.

1.4.2 Step-by-Step Remote Support: A quick google survey (Figure 1.6) was done of students who possessed devices of their own, had access to internet, had the required bandwidth and support and alternate modes of engagement were decided for the limited numbers who had difficulty in accessing these lectures.

MS teams recording was sent by whatsapp to these students, till they found alternate methods of adapting to the remote instruction system. The following are the parametres that were used for assessing the student reach to internet connectivity and that which formed the base for deciding the pedagogy to be employed and the teaching-learning resources to be deployed.

- Satisfaction of Digital Initiatives undertaken
- Access to Devices
- Internet connectivity
- Attendance during Online classes
- Optional Mode of classes
- Continuity as a hosteller
- Online assessments
- Readiness to take up the new normal
- Parent opinion

Figure 1.6: Parameters

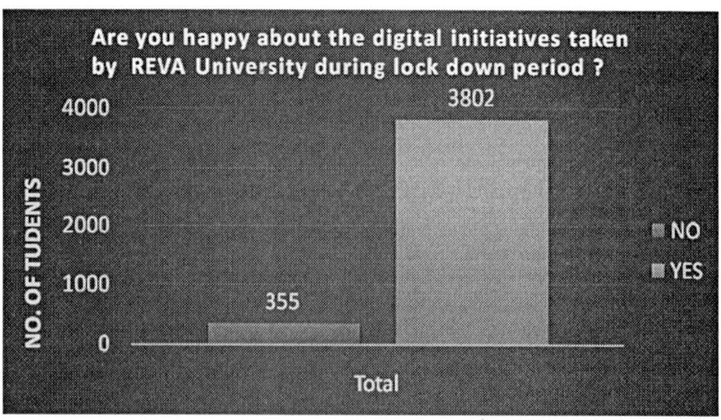

Google survey forms (Figure 1.7) which were shared with students also included feedback on classes, clarity in presentation, assignment and evaluation feedback. The feedback received was collated and after quality check and review, shared with the concerned faculty.

Figure 1.7: Google Survey Forms

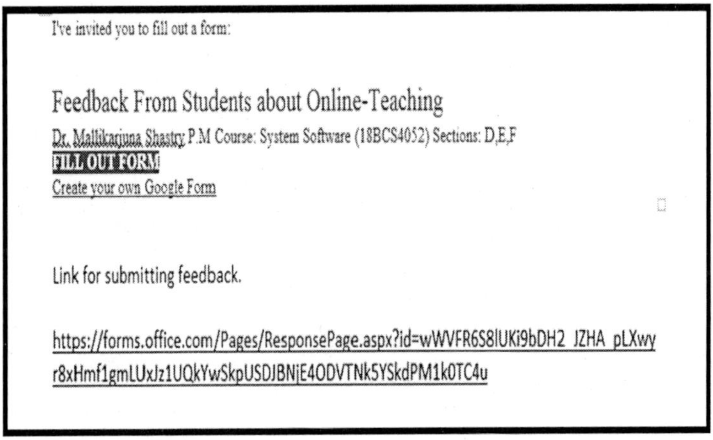

I've invited you to fill out a form:

Feedback From Students about Online-Teaching

Dr. Mallikarjuna Shastry P.M Course: System Software (18BCS4052) Sections: D,E,F

FILL OUT FORM

Create your own Google Form

Link for submitting feedback.

https://forms.office.com/Pages/ResponsePage.aspx?id=wWVFR6S8lUKi9bDH2_JZHA_pLXwyr8xHmf1gmLUxJz1UQkYwSkpUSDJBNjE4ODVTNk5YSkdPM1k0TC4u

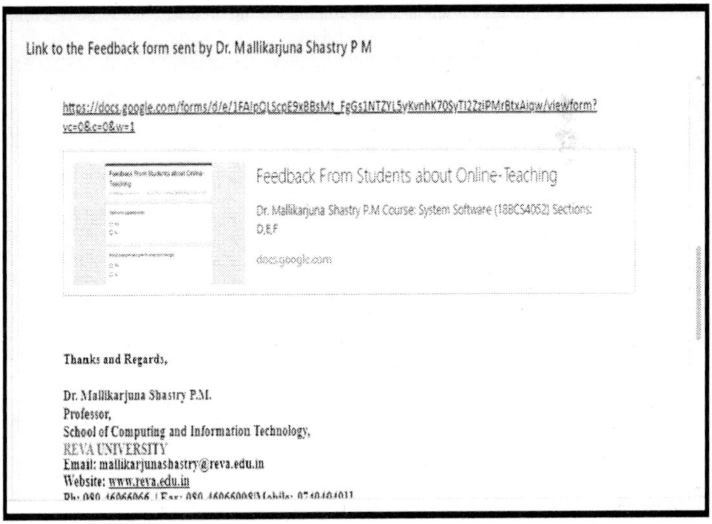

Link to the Feedback form sent by Dr. Mallikarjuna Shastry P M

https://docs.google.com/forms/d/e/1FAIpQLScpE9xBBsMt_FgGs1NTZYL5yKvnhK70SyTI2ZziPMrBtxAiqw/viewform?vc=0&c=0&w=1

Feedback From Students about Online-Teaching

Dr. Mallikarjuna Shastry P.M Course: System Software (18BCS4052) Sections: D,E,F

docs.google.com

Thanks and Regards,

Dr. Mallikarjuna Shastry P.M.
Professor,
School of Computing and Information Technology,
REVA UNIVERSITY
Email: mallikarjunashastry@reva.edu.in
Website: www.reva.edu.in

1.4.3 Rescheduling: The School Time Tables were revised and core subjects were given emphasis to in terms of number of hours for teaching. The revised time table was shared with all students (Figure 1.8).

Figure 1.8: Online Teaching Time Tables

Online Teaching Timetable for Academic year 2019-20 (Even Semester, Assignment Hours of 8hrs/Week for Credit)				
School Name : School of Mechanical Engineering				Program Name : B Tech
Semester : VI				Section : A to E
Day	Time	9.30 AM to 10.30 AM	12 Noon to 1 PM	3 PM to 4 PM
Wednesday	Subject Name	Finite Element Method /Turbo Machines	Heat and Mass Trasfer /Theory of Machines-II	CAD/CAM
	Faculty Name	DSA, SSS/CDH, SG, MBP	KKM, VR/SPB, HR, RSC	BS/PSK/LNS/DM/RBS
	Section	A,B /C,D,E	A,B /C,D,E	A,B,C,D,E
Thursday	Subject Name	Machine Design-II	Soft Core-1 Refrigeration & Air conditioning, Manufacturing Technology-III,Production Planning & Control,Theory of Elasticity	Soft Core-2 Renewable Energy Resources, Mechatronics& Microprocessor,Industrial Engineering
	Faculty Name	SPS,VK, SNS,RKR, MNG	LRJ,ABK,NNSB,AMV,CNK,SGS	RT,VT,MC,ML,AKH,PSK
	Section	A,B,C,D,E	A,B,C,D,E	A,B,C,D,E
Friday	Subject Name	Finite Element Method /Turbo Machines	Heat and Mass Trasfer /Theory of Machines-II	CAD/CAM
	Faculty Name	DSA, SSS/CDH, SG, MBP	KKM, VR/SPB, HR, RSC	BS/PSK/LNS/DM/RBS
	Section	A,B /C,D,E	A,B /C,D,E	A,B,C,D,E
Saturday	Subject Name	Machine Design-II	Soft Core-1 Refrigeration & Air conditioning, Manufacturing Technology-III,Production Planning & Control,Theory of Elasticity	Soft Core-2 Renewable Energy Resources, Mechatronics& Microprocessor,Industrial Engineering
	Faculty Name	SPS,VK, SNS,RKR, MNG	LRJ,ABK,NNSB,AMV,CNK,SGS	RT,VT,MC,ML,AKH,PSK
	Section	A,B,C,D,E	A,B,C,D,E	A,B,C,D,E

1.4.4 Restructuring: MS Teams was the platform used by most faculty and the wireframe of support to all schools in terms of training for those who were not used to using Teams and also wireframe of support to all classes was prepared. A quick illustration of the same would enable understanding of the structure employed (Figure 1.9).

Figure 1.9: : Wireframe

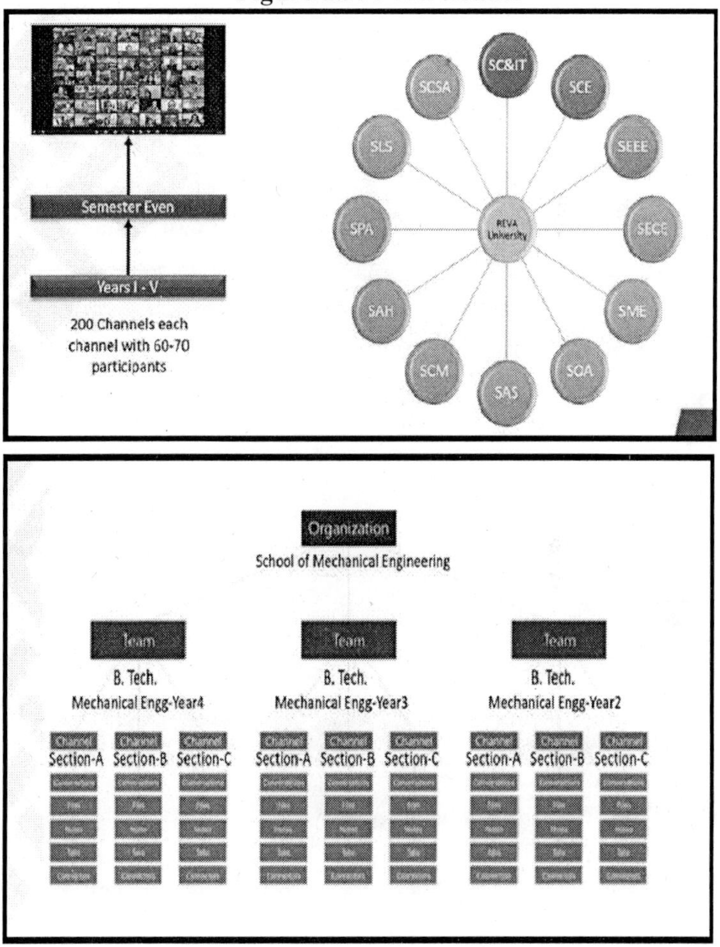

During various meetings held by me personally and also by individual School Directors, faculty were coached on recording of their sessions, attending to student queries using MS Teams (Figure 1.10). New set of guidelines were issued to faculty on how to go about their sessions, while students were shared small tips and instructions for class readiness and responses. Mentors were also groomed to ensure that mentoring sessions were conducted periodically and students were given tips on staying home, calming the mind, composure and above all physical wellness and academic focus. The following are the screen shots taken for illustration of how these sessions were conducted remotely and also from campus of faculty who resided in the campus.

Figure 1.10: Screenshots of MS Teams Classes

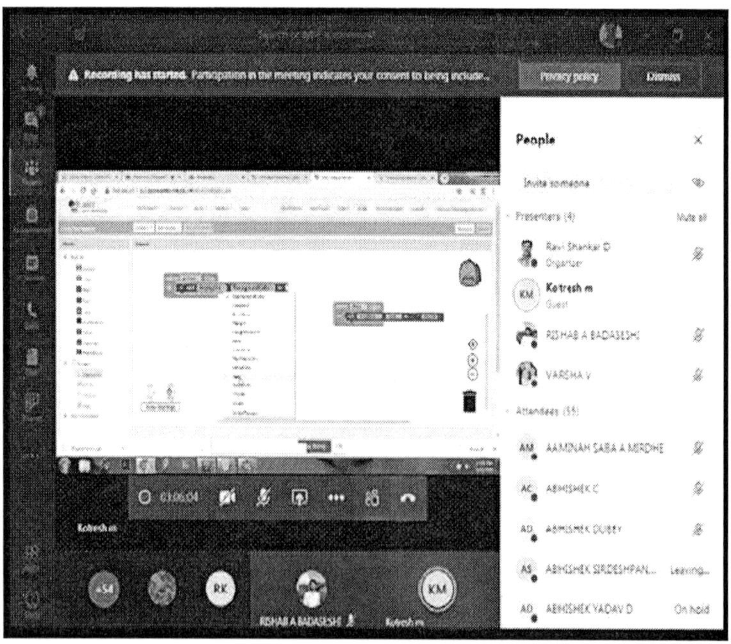

Figure 1.10: Screenshots of MS Teams Classes

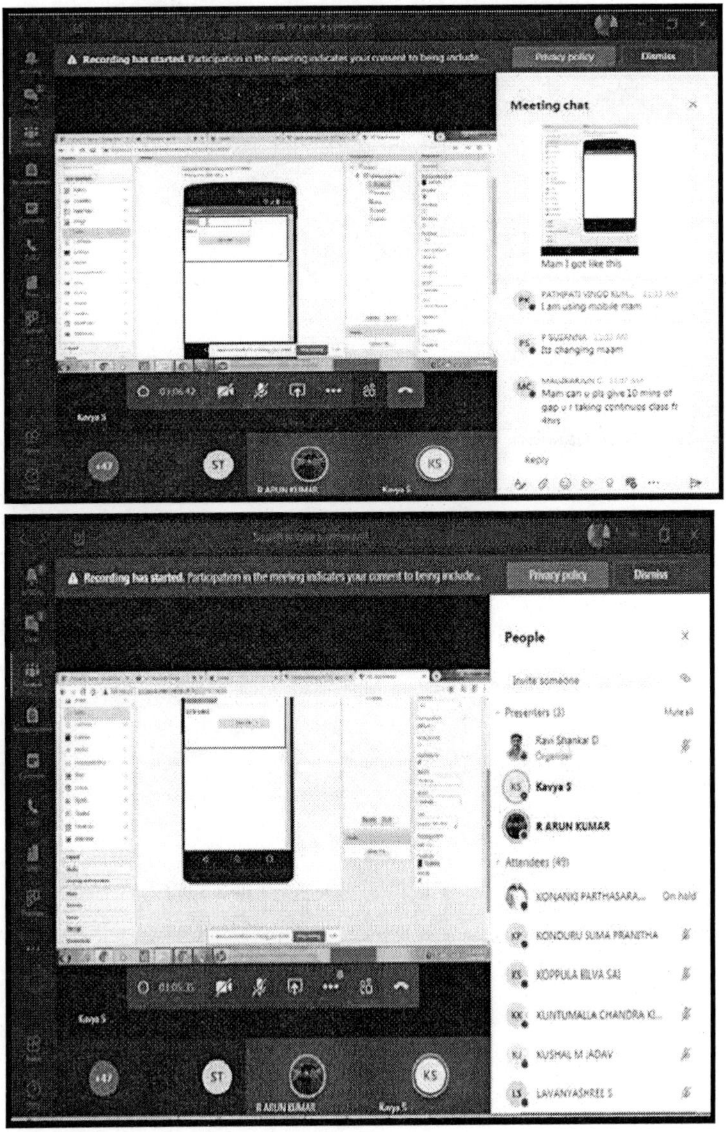

Feedback of these classes conducted online (Figure 1.11) was prime and students were given the liberty to write back to their Directors, talk to their faculty and also fill in the survey form for feedback on their classes conducted online.

The IQAC team at the University sat through recorded sessions and also participated in these classes, to ensure that there was quality check and measures were in place to plough back feedback to the concerned faculty.

Figure 1.11: Feedback of Classes

From: D.V.S. Bhagavanulu bhagavanulu@gmail.com
Sent: Thursday, April 23, 2020 4:02 PM
To: Dr. Surendra Rao Shankapal <shankapal@reva.edu.in>;
Subject: Fwd: Links of Recorded Online lectures

Sir,

Greetings

The following points were observed from the online lectures delivered by the faculty of REVA University and feedback given to all Directors as below: ***

1. Your faculty have followed the timetable strictly.
2. Most of the faculty used power point presentations during their lectures, please do encourage them to use other resources as well
3. Question and answer sessions have been arranged at the end of the lecture to the students.
4. Very few faculty have not used white board
5. The audio and video quality is good in most of the lectures
6. Nearly 90% of the students have accessed live streaming of the lectures every day.
7. Please ensure that after completion of the lecture, the recorded lectures are kept in library files for the students to access again and for the students who missed the lectures for various reasons.
8. Please ensure all the faulty send their material to their respective email id.
9. All doubts of students have to be clarified.
10. Please ensure assignments are graded and shared in time with students
11. Feedback is taken from the students and observed that they are quite satisfied with the delivery and content of the material.
12. It is observed from the live streaming of classes that more than 85% of the students are attending the classes.

For any clarifications, please revert to me.

Regards
Dr D VS Bhagavanulu

As quality initiative from the Management of REVA University, recorded lectures of the faculty was collected randomly and the quality cell also followed the live streaming of the lectures in MS teams.

Name of the faculty	Links
Dr. Nagaraja V	https://web.microsoftstream.com/video/ce809b18-178e-4940-b699-f06fc654ee3c
Dr. Ranjeet Mohanty	https://web.microsoftstream.com/video/e18ce231-95e2-4d53-8e3d-1f0e4bc58448
Dr. Kumara	https://web.microsoftstream.com/video/8af4873a-c48e-4e26-a8f5-ca6c57912d00
Prof. Raghavendra G	https://web.microsoftstream.com/video/316b910d-e963-44cb-93b5-766f43329994

At the same time, the Management also took interest in ensuring that there was seamless delivery of all classes and quality checks were in place and ensured some of the sessions were attended to personally which also included me sitting through some sessions.

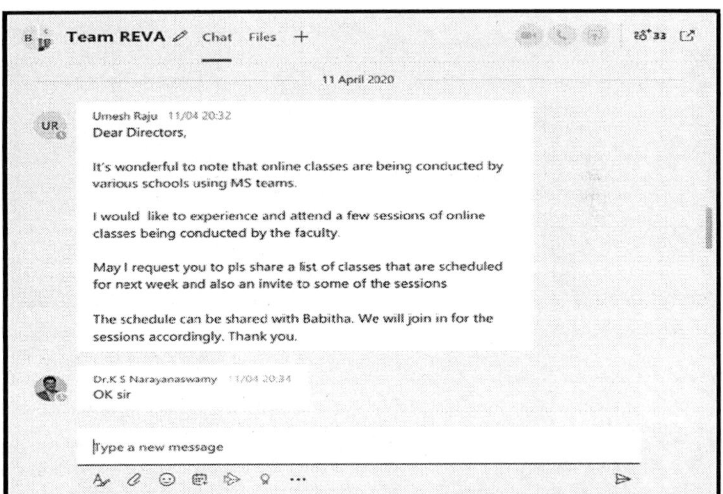

The ERP team ensured that feedback from students was taken and the parameters for this included (Figure 1.12):

- Clarity and accessibility of online classes on Ms Teams
- Course material support
- Coverage of syllabus at appropriate pace
- Regularity and punctuality
- Delivery of online lectures
- Communication of faculty
- Continuous Assessments and Assignments
- Working beyond scheduled hours
- Mentoring

FEEDBACK REPORT

Sl.No	SRN	NAME	Preparedness and delivery during online classes in MS Teams	Communication and teaching skills of the subject teachers during online classes	punctuality of subject teachers for taking online class	Continuous assessment of assignments and quizzes	Preparation and distribution of course materials for prescribed syllabus	Availability and response of faculty members in clearing doubts during online classes	Syllabus coverage through online session	subject teachers interaction and relationship with students during online classes	STUDENT COMMENT
1	R18CV231	SHREYAS S.	3	3	5	5	1	5	3	5	Facing network problem
2	R19CV176	FIRAS HANEEF GHOURI	3	4	5	5	2	3	3	3	Good
3	R19CV177	HARI MANIKANTA P.	5	5	5	5	5	5	5	5	Good
4	R19CV178	HARIN GOWDA K C.	4	5	4	4	5	5	5	5	No comments
5	R19CV179	HARSHITHA TR	3	4	5	4	4	3	3	3	Satisfactory
6	R19CV180	HEMA H.	3	3	3	3	4	4	4	3	Network issue
7	R19CV181	JAGADISH S.	5	5	5	5	5	5	5	5	Excellent
8	R19CV182	JEEVAN S N	-	-	-	-	-	-	-		
9	R19CV183	K H SUDEEP.	5	5	5	5	5	5	5	5	No comments

Figure 1.12: Feedback Captured

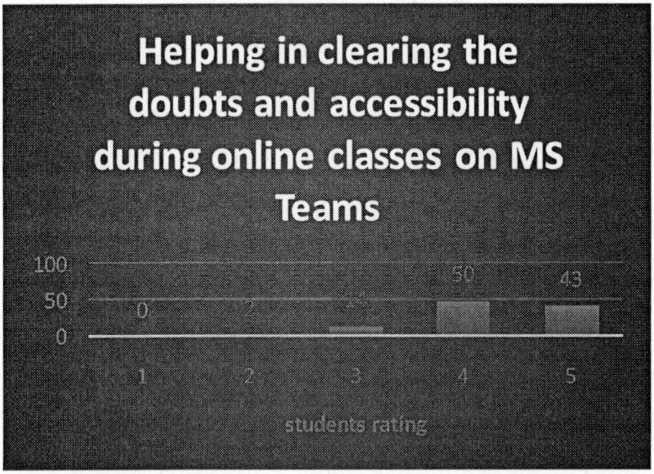

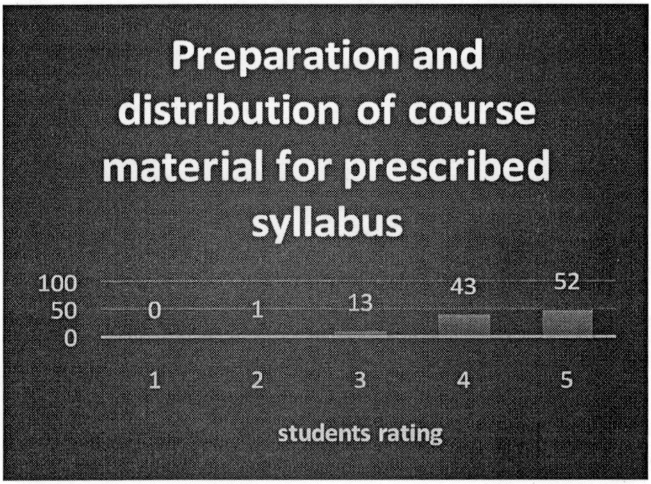

1.5 Mentoring

At REVA it has been a mandatory practice to counsel students and each faculty is assigned a batch of 10-15 students for mentoring (Figure 1.13).

This practice continued even during COVID as mentors spoke and counselled their mentees using MS Teams sessions and also documented the progress of the students.

This way the connect between the mentor-mentee and students counselling during these anxious times was retained.

Figure 1.13: Mentor - Mentee Sessions

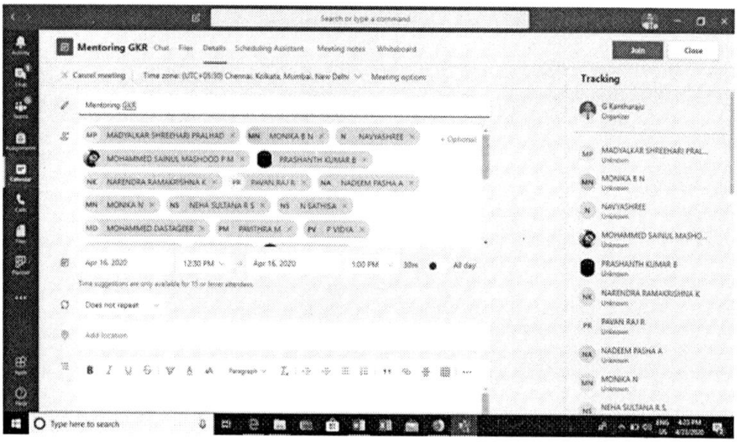

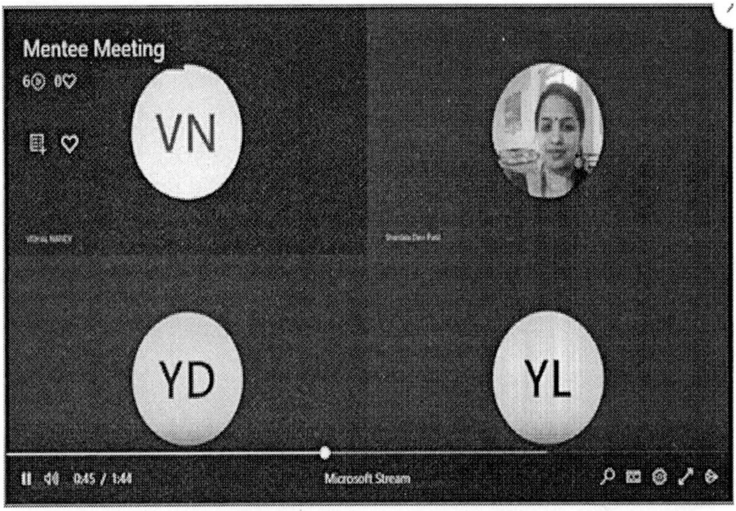

Figure 1.13: Mentor Meetings

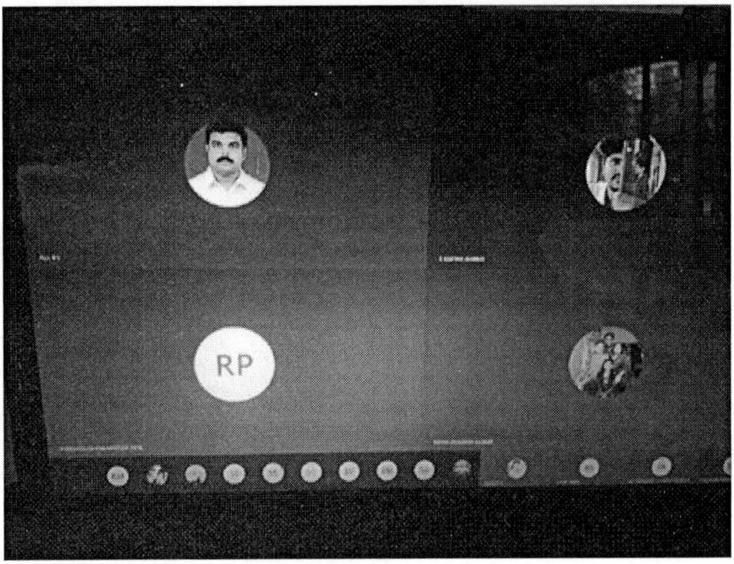

1.6 REVA Academy for Corporate Excellence (RACE)

1.6.1 RACE Launched Virtual Classrooms for Seamless Virtual Learning during the Pandemic. Due to the outbreak of COVID-19 pandemic, as per the government directives and given the safety of our corporate program participants and mentors, REVA University and REVA Academy for Corporate Excellence (RACE), had suspended all the classroom training sessions from March 14th and transitioned seamlessly into a virtual learning environment with a motto of "Learning Never Stops".

RACE programs, being technical, lab-driven, the RACE team put together a completely virtual environment to run online classes in emerging technologies like Data Science, Artificial Intelligence and Cyber Security. Three major pillars of this online delivery at RACE include:

1. Remote connection to RACE's State-of-the-Art Labs through a secured VPN and RDP.
2. Live online sessions with industry mentors through MS-Teams/Zoom/WEBEX.
3. 24/7 support through a customised Learning Management System integrated with Live sessions.

1.6.2 Setting-up the Remote Infrastructure through Secured VPN and RDP: The specialised executive programs in Cybersecurity and Analytics programs require hands-on sessions on the segregated environment and hence remote access to the labs has been a critical ingredient for the successful delivery of online learning in its true sense. To facilitate the labs remotely, the RACE team set up a secured Virtual Private Network (VPN) to access the Data and Proprietary software at the campus. A few of the software were given cloud access. Remote Desktop Protocols (RDP) are created and access is given to all the participants. This remote access has been a truly differentiating factor and made all the practical lab sessions go online without a glitch.

1.6.3 Live Online Sessions with Industry Mentors through MS-Teams/Zoom/WEBEX: RACE uses multiple virtual platforms like MS Teams / WEBEX / Zoom efficiently to conduct all the online sessions. Mentors connected remotely with the learners through these platforms to conduct interactive sessions through video conferencing. MS Teams with its various integrated tools like, fully integrated Office 365, conversational channels, Onedrive, Sharepoint, Whiteboard, Planners etc. were used extensively not just for the sessions, but also for connecting with fellow learners outside the formal sessions bringing the real joy of collaborative efforts and teamwork.

RACE has customised the curriculum, empathising with the online learner which was well appreciated. The RACE participants experienced a seamless learning environment as the team provided all the functions of a normal classroom environment including labs and theory sessions without diluting the quality of academic delivery.

1.6.4 24/7 Support with Learning Management System Integrating Virtual Sessions: The participants were provided more individual support during the lock-down. Additional sessions, labs and live interactions with mentors are provided to keep up the learning spirit. The online lecture videos were recorded on a real-time basis and made available in the Learning Management System of RACE so that the learners can refer to those videos for future learning or clarifying their doubts. The assignments and assessments were scheduled periodically using Safe Browser Mode and Virtual Monitoring Tools to ensure the sanctity of the examinations.

1.6.5 Happy Customers and Happy Learning: The learners of RACE's academic programs, who are also working professionals with several years of industry experience in their respective domains found these online classroom sessions helpful, informative and interesting.

According to Joy Ramachandran, Head of Practice Database Technology, SAP Labs and participant of M. Tech in Cybersecurity said on his social media handle, "Attending the ongoing weekend M. Tech classes from 10 am to 6 pm. It is tough to look at the monitor from the morning for a long 8 hours. But the quality was superb! Thanks to our professor and the entire backend IT staff of RACE and REVA University. Other Universities across the world can also try this innovative method rather than cancelling classes. Stay at home and make it meaningful!"

For REVA Academy for Corporate Excellence (RACE), going virtual was as easy as flipping a coin, since we are pro-active in creating some of the state-of-the-art technology stacks and world-class mentors which makes learning a truly gratifying experience irrespective of the circumstances.

Figure 1.14: SDC Courses

Semester and Branch	Title of the Course	Total Enrolments	Active Enrolments	Completions
VI Semester B.Tech (CSE) VI Semester B.Tech (ECE) VI Semester B.Tech (Civil) VI Semester B.Tech (Mechanical) VI Semester B.Tech (EEE) VI Semester B.Sc (Research) IV Semester BCA MCA M.S in CS	Java Programming: Solving Problems with Software	1774	1245	336
	Object Oriented Programming in Java	1096	793	121
	Java Programming: Arrays, Lists, and Structured Data	250	79	9
	Object-Oriented Programming with Java	27	18	5
	Java for Android	25	14	2
	Interactivity with JavaScript	19	11	3
	Java Programming: Principles of Software Design	26	6	0
VIII Semester BA and BBA LL.B	Building your Leadership skills	67	56	27
VIII Semester B.Arch	Entrepreneurship strategy : From ideation to exit	61	52	46
II Semester MBA	Introduction to Business Analytics : Communicating with Data	272	255	249
II Semester M.Com	Financial Markets	25	15	1
	Introduction to Financial Markets	37	33	30
IV Semester B.Com and BBA	Fundamentals of Visualization with Tableau	529	523	482
IV Semester B.A (JEP) II Semester M.A (Journalism and Mass communication)	Digital Media and Marketing Strategies	103	99	92
II Semester M.Sc (Physics) II Semester M.Sc (Maths)	Python Basics	93	73	47
II Semester M.Sc (Bio-Chem)	Finding Hidden Messages in DNA (Bioinformatics I)	45	44	30

1.7 University Industry Interaction Centre (UIIC)

The University Industry Interaction Centre supports the entire University with skill based certification programmes and aligns all programmes with the industry. All Skill Development courses were mapped with Coursera for Campus and students in the senior semesters were given free licences to ensure that the required and planned skill development certificate programmes were conducted as scheduled (Figure 1.14).

1.7.1 Coursera for Campus: Regular tracking was done of all the certificate programs that were on offer to students and the following is a glimpse of how these sessions were tracked (Figure 1.15).

Figure 1.15: Coursera for Campus Tracked

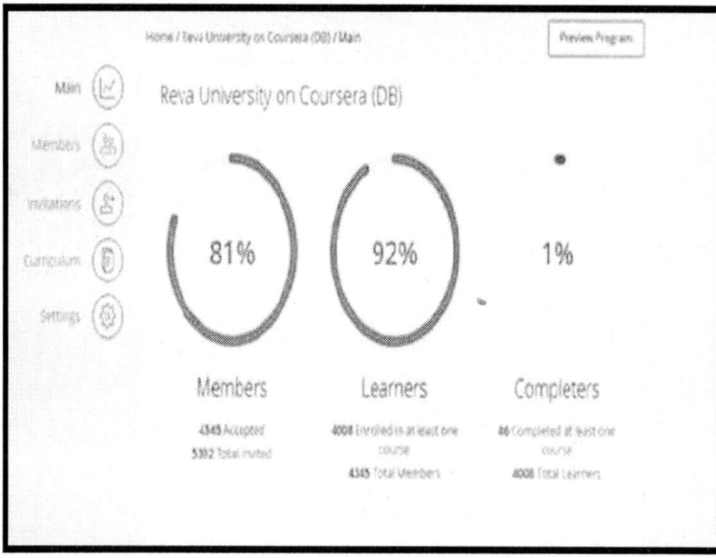

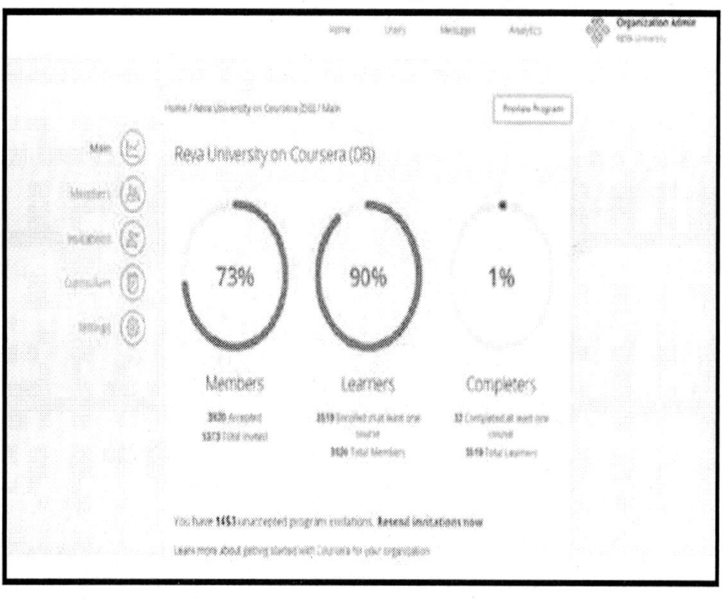

1.8 REVA NEST

REVA NEST and UIIC was not to be left behind during these times and the team took it upon themselves to support students and young entrepreneurs as they initiated the COVID-19 Digital Campaign. The initiative by the University was to spread awareness about COVID-19 and disseminate the right information about Coronavirus among Citizens. E-Certificates were given to participants and nearly 3,300 participants took up the online Awareness Digital Campaign and E-Certification.

The main aim of such courses was to provide awareness to the citizens regarding the precautions to be taken by people to safeguard themselves as well as people around them from COVID-19 and make a difference in fighting against this pandemic.The course materials and quiz was aimed to provide information about social distancing, precautions, flattening the curve, self-care instructions as well as to keep oneself aware and hence make a difference (Figure 1.16).

Figure 1.16: Building Awareness of COVID

1.8.1 REVA Code Lab: REVA CodeLab is a technical upskilling app developed by collaboration between REVA NEST and School of C&IT, REVA University to keep the coding abilities of students on fleek by improving their coding skills in C, C++, Java and Python (Figure 1.17).

The application consists of thousands of MCQ's of each programming language in "Practice Test" option where a student can take tests of 10 random MCQs at a time to test their abilities and improve their skills.

The application specifies if the student has selected a wrong answer and provides the correct answer during the test.

Figure 1.17: Building Coding Skills

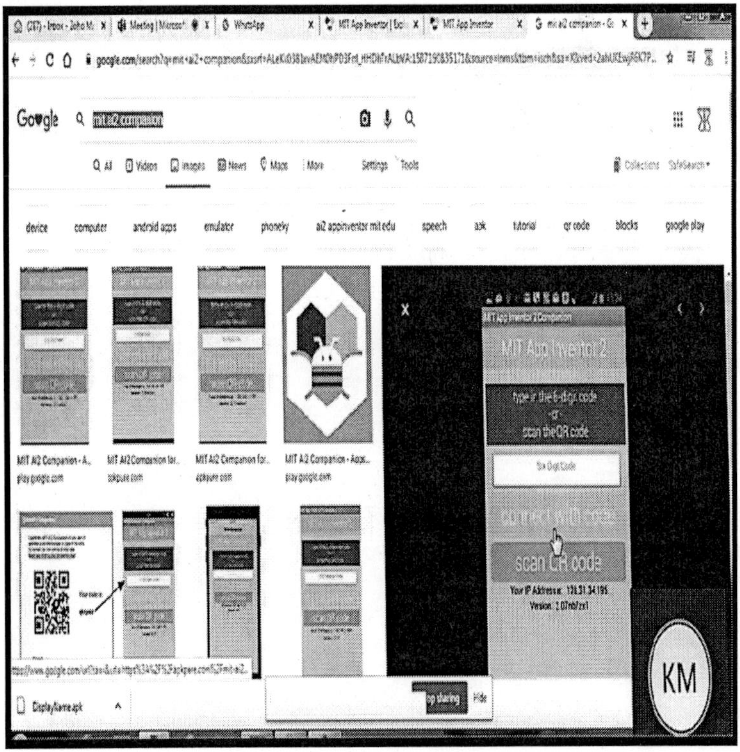

Figure 1.17: Building Coding Skills

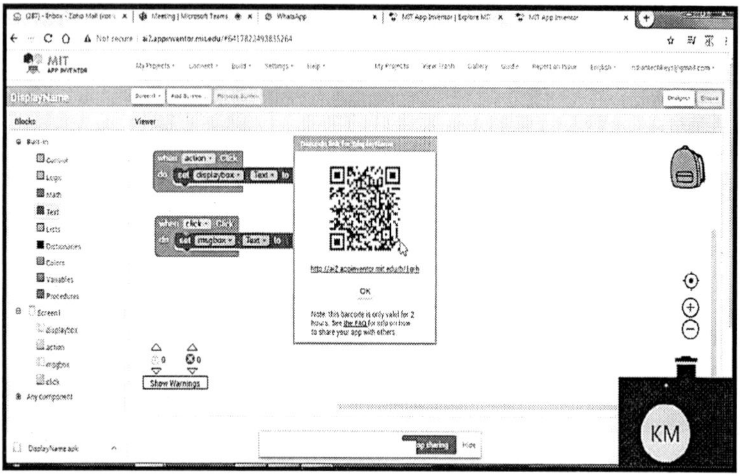

Coursera for Campus

Apart from this, REVA UIIC was quick to offer Coursera for Campus courses to the final semester students to build on their skills development and also enrich their portfolios to make them employable by the industry. These courses were also offered to the batch of Afghan students who had to leave the country due to this situation and who needed remote assistance the most.

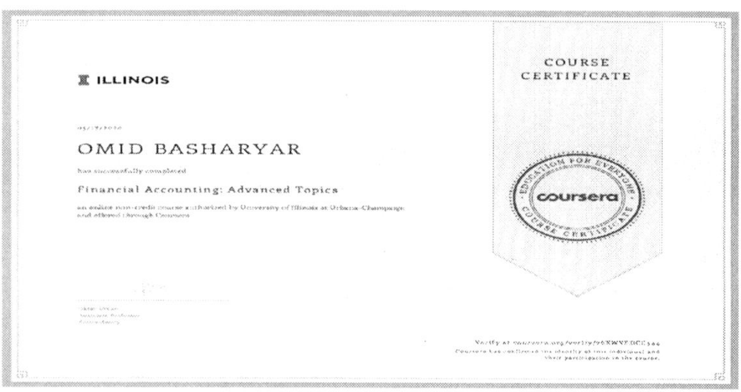

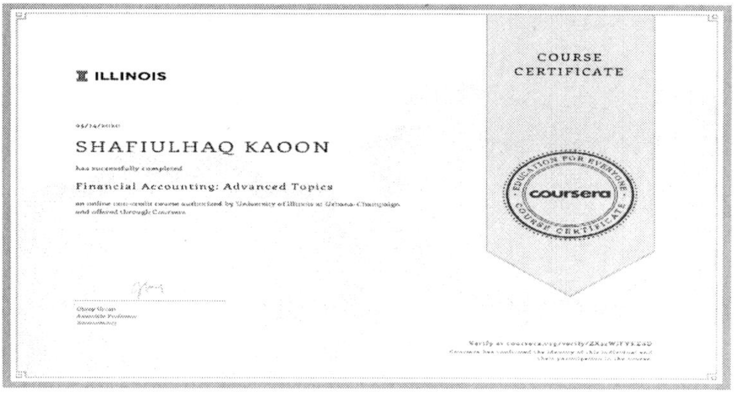

1.9 Career Development Centre

The Career Development Centre at REVA supported the students during COVID. Since most of the placements were over for the cycle, students who were already placed grew anxious of their appointments. It was important to ensure that they were counselled and also spoken to periodically so that their minds were calm. Students who were interning with various companies were counselled over phone, on MS Teams sessions and assured that their positions in the companies where they were recruited was intact. At the same time, if offers were revoked by some companies due to the COVID impact, the team was quick to ensure that an alternate job offer was made to the student concerned.

1.10 Research and Innovation Connect

The Research and Innovation team at REVA focussed on keeping the morale of scholars high during these times. They ensured mails were consistently sent to scholars and tips on research related activities were dated. The Dean with the support from IT team, created official IDs for the scholars with the intention of conducting review meetings on line. Several scholars who were on the verge of thesis submission, were given assurance that the University was in a position to conduct the online review meetings at any time after the permission from UGC was granted. As promised, the University began to conduct the online reviews to the satisfaction of the scholars (Figure 1.18).

Figure 1.18: Communique with Ph.D. Scholars

From: Coordinator PHD <coordtphd@reva.edu.in>
Sent: 2 April 2020 13:36
To: Dr. B P Divakar <divakar@reva.edu.in>
Cc: Dr. Surendra Rao Shankapal <sharkapal@reva.edu.in>; Dr. Dhanamjaya M <registrar@reva.edu.in>; Dr. Ramachandra P <registrarevaluation@reva.edu.in>
Subject: PhD Program 2020 Batch ...

Dear Applicants,

GREETINGS FROM REVA UNIVERSITY

Thank you for your interest in selecting RU for your Ph.D program. The unforeseen situation has made us to delay the conduction of the (PET) test. We have options open to both on and off-line examinations for which preliminary preparations have been completed. Minimal exposure and taking care of health is of paramount important to us at the moment. Tentatively, it has been scheduled in the month of July with the hope to commence the course in September. The mode of conduction will be decided and communicated later depending on the prevailing conditions. Request you to be patient and concentrate on the proposal to be submitted during your counseling.

PS:
For online, you should have laptop/desktop with webcam which will have to enabled during the entire session. Further instructions shall follow in due course of time.

Warm Regards,

Dr. B P Divakar
Dean | Research and Innovation Council
Mobile: +91 9108635754

The COVID-19 situation saved travelling time and made working from home truly productive for researchers and faculty members. A decision was taken to raise the bar of expectations on publications considering the situation and accordingly the targets were revised and communicated which was taken positively by members (Figure 1.19).

Several webinars and interdisciplinary lectures were arranged online for the benefits of the members.

Figure 1.19: Research Support

From: Dr. B.P Divakar <divakar@reva.edu.in>
Sent: 02 April 2020 13:44
To: All <all@reva.edu.in>
Subject: Fw: research repository.

Dear all

Please refer to the link mentioned and access the research repository for your research.
https://ndl.iitkgp.ac.in/

National Digital Library of India

National Digital Library of India Project Central Library (ISO-9001:2015 Certified) Indian Institute of Technology Kharagpur Kharagpur India - 721302. Phone: +91-3222-282435. For any issue or feedback, please write to ndl-support@iitkgp.ac.in

ndl.iitkgp.ac.in

https://ndl.iitkgp.ac.in/corona-research/scholar

Warm Regards,

Dr. B P Divakar

Dean | Research and Innovation Council

Mobile: +91 9108635754

1.11 Assessments and Online Evaluation

We were quick to adapt to the online examinations for final assessment as well. Online examination has been planned in a timely phase and since REVA follows a paperless exam mode, it was easier for students to adapt themselves to the online assessments plan. Based on the google survey done earlier, it was easier to identify the students who had concerns with internet and they were given alternate solutions.

Quick steps were taken to draw up guidelines for students after a series of meetings conducted inhouse with Directors and it was unanimously conveyed to all students with the website carrying clear cut directions on the conducting of the exams (Figure 1.20).

The vendor selection was made based on parameters such as: features of the exams, proctored and non-proctored, security of exams, authenthication, question type support, support in drawings and devices, remote and digital proctoring features, security, audit trail, disruptions and support and other parameters.

Figure 1.20: Revised Guidelines for Exams

REVA UNIVERSITY

SEMESTER END EXAMINATIONS MAY - JUNE 2020

Preamble: The Semester End Examinations (SEE) of II, IV, VI, VIII, X semesters of various programmes that come under different faculties of REVA University are scheduled during the months of May and June 2020. The SEEs conducted will have certain deviations in the mode of conduct of examinations, pattern of question papers and overall weightage distribution between continuous assessments and SEE from the University Examination Regulations due to Covid-19 Pandemic.

UGC Guidelines on Examinations:

One may refer "UGC Guidelines on Examinations and Academic Calendar for the Universities in View of COVID-19 Pandemic and Subsequent Lockdown", D.O.No. F. 1-1/2020(Secy) dated 29th April 2020.

As per the guidelines, REVA University has decided to conduct **Semester End Examinations (SEE)** through online mode, using Multiple Choice Question (MCQ) pattern of question paper. Each such examination will be held for a duration of 2 hours and for a maximum of 60 marks. The weightage distribution for deciding grade in each course is 70% for continuous assessment (assessed through assignments, quizzes, tests) and 30% for SEE conducted online.

The online examination will be administered through a Third Party who has expertise in conducting online examinations to various corporates and Universities.

Online Examination Guidelines for Students:

Online examinations are scheduled from 27th of May 2020.

Students will receive an email with the final exam link from admin@mettl.com on their REVA Email ID.

Instructions regarding online examinations:

System Requirements

1. It is recommended that you take the exam in the latest versions of Firefox or Chrome browser for

1.11.1 Guidelines on the Website

Mock testing was done for students and hall tickets were generated accordingly.

Figure 1.21: Hall Tickets

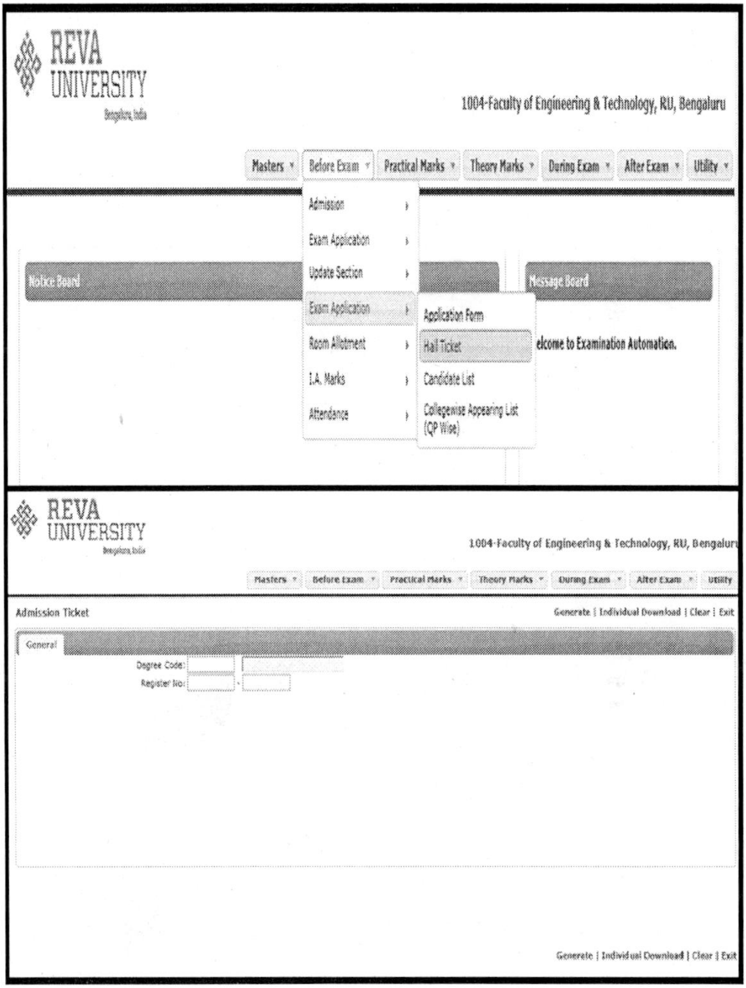

1.12 At the Campus

1.12.1 Halls of Residences: The safey of our resident staff grew to be a major challenge as student parents and guardians were worried just as all in the campus were worried. In the initial few days when the fear of the virus had just begun, all the staff of concerned schools took it upon themselves to supervise and work along with the hostellers to keep their rooms clean and also fumigate all the rooms on a regular basis.

Food habits were checked and I personally addressed the students so as to ensure that they followed all the guidelines given.

Figure 1.22: Cleaning of Hostels

At this point communication with all parents was crucial and hence all resident wardens took it upon themselves to stay in constant touch with parents. While students were sent back safely to their homes and this was followed by frequent calls to check on their welfare and health, wardens also ensured that students were advised to attend the online classes regularly, take their online tests seriously, stay safe and alert while in their home town. At the hostels, we took it upon ourselves to ensure all their belongings were safely stashed inside their rooms.Arrangements were made to pick the books/laptops and deliver them to the local students. Students were asked to report to the concerned authority if there was any issue that they faced and assurance given that the hostels would be safe for students when they return to campus.

Figure 1.23: Housekeepers Alerted

1.12.2 Preventive Measures: Immediate measures at the campus was priority and it was important that the campus was spruced and geared to take care of the immediate safety of the staff and students. Engagement drives were conducted with the team. All housekeeping staff were educated to begin with so that they were cautioned and alerted. Preventive measures counted in the campus and we went ahead and started work with the team.

1.12.3 Social Distancing and Staff Meeting: Faculty meetings were conducted in the campus keeping social distancing in mind and resident staff were alerted and briefed on security measures.

Figure 1.24: Faculty Meetings

Parent Communique

Parents and student were sent letters by ERP so that they were briefed about what was happening in campus.

Figure 1.25: Mailers to Parents

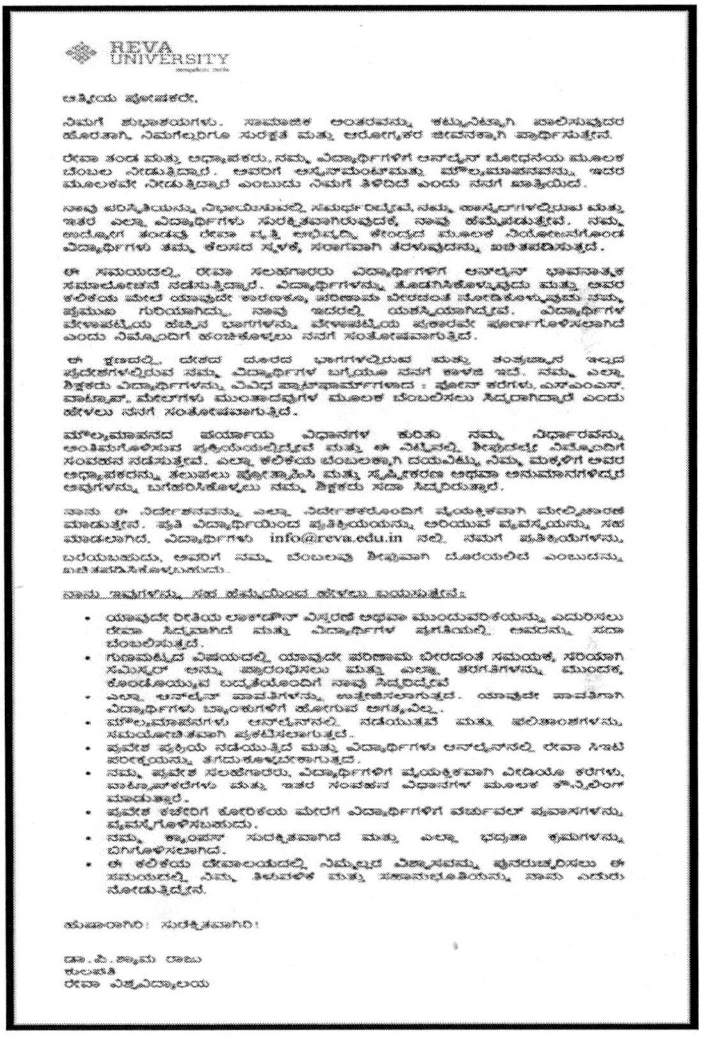

REVA UNIVERSITY
Bengaluru, India
Established as per the section 2(f) of the UGC Act, 1956
Approved by AICTE, COA and BCI, New Delhi

Dear all

Greetings from REVA University!

As we are all aware we are facing unprecedented times as the world gets together to respond to the COVID-19 pandemic. At REVA, it has been our commitment to maintain the health and safety of our students, faculty and communities. While is not very clear what the challenges in the upcoming days and weeks will be, I am sure lockdown is not the only medicine for corona virus. Lockdown is only a systemic control brought out by the Government to control the virus from spreading, to bring in awareness and seriousness amongst people. At the same time, the Government or the Management of REVA has no control over the virus. As of date as we are all aware, there is no medicine or relief from this virus. The responsibility of controlling the virus from spreading lies in our hands. It is my responsibility and yours to stay safe. What we need to immediately do is to change our lifestyle maintain social distance, build our immunity levels, avoid junk food, eat healthy and nutritious food. Above all, it is our will power that can save us. Growing responsible for our own family, for our kith and kin and more than anything performing our duties and roles with care and precaution is what is the need of the hour. Life has changed and we need to accept this change. While I send you our warm wishes, we only hope that you and your family remain healthy and safe during these challenging times. Thank you for your continued patience, understanding and support as we at REVA navigate through the crisis along with you. We are confident that we will emerge from this difficult times and will deliver our continued commitment towards education and strengthen the future.

We are continuing to accept applications for incoming academic year and have begun processing the applications that we have already received. We are very flexible with late applications and will accept late applications given the circumstances we are in. We will be as communicative as possible with you and our students during these days.

God bless!

Dr P. Shyama Raju
Chancellor
REVA University

Display Boards

COVID alert boards were quickly mounted in all strategic locations in the campus.

Figure 1.26: Signages

Jagruti towards COVID-19: REVA immediately started a digital campaign towards awareness and defence against COVID-19 and this was our contribution towards creating an awareness towards COVID-19 (Jagruti towards COVID-19). Students were consistently reminded to wear clean and fresh clothes, sanitize even the lanyard where they wear their ID cards, encouraged to use namaste against a handshake, avoid body contact and maintain safe distance while hanging out in the campus. Sanitizers were placed in strategic points in the campus. In fact our School of Applied Sciences went ahead and prepared smaller dispensers of hand wash in our labs so that students had access to these sanitizers liberally. The campus was generous with use of tissues and our medical centre was equipped with care which ranges from masks to a tie up with medical labs. We began promoting safe travel and car poolers were alerted and given safety tips. Most of all, students were warned though our digital boards to stay away from fear mongering and to maintain normalcy in the campus. REVA set an example for others to follow.

The resident staff took part in all the PM campaigns and alerts that were shared.

Figure 1.27: Janatha Curfew

Figure 1.27: Janatha Curfew

Figure 1.28: Diya Jalao

Fumigation: Buses were fumigated immediately and sanitizers were placed in all wash rooms as well as entry and exit points of each block.

Figure 1.29: Care of Travel

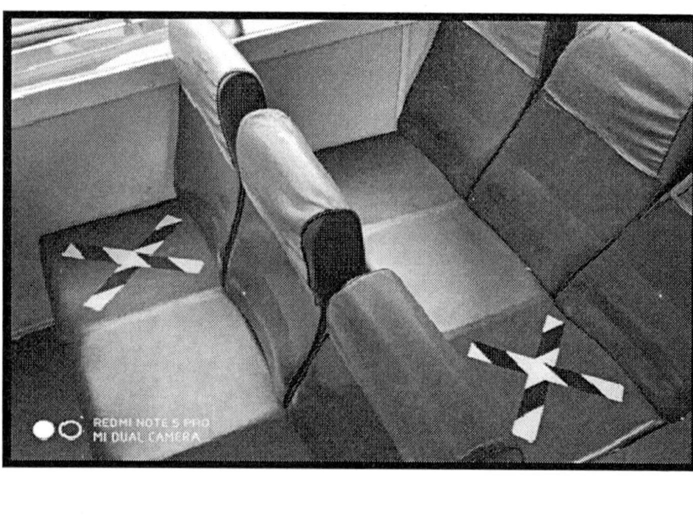

The NCC and NSS teams started work with the local bodies and the cadets worked with all bodies starting from the police to the BBMP to ensure that they were supported in all ways.

Social media campaigns grew powerful and we worked to build this awareness amongst the public as part of the University Social Responsibility.

I personally started attending TV interviews so that our messaging was shared across various demographies and we could share our learning and readiness with other institutions who could pace their strategies.

Figure 1.30: At TV Studios

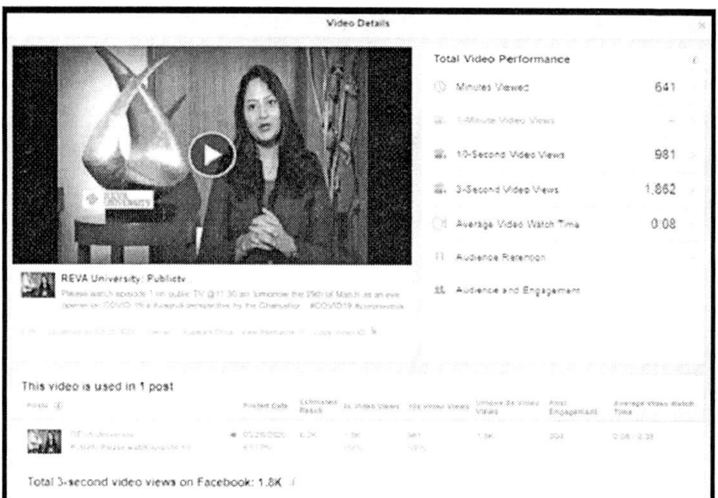

1.13 Working towards Society

REVA University was quick to rise to the occasion and support the community at large during COVID-19 times from limited access to resources and materials to limited transport facility and manual safety; the staff and select students quickly put their thoughts together and the Chemistry lab along with REVA UIIC kept sanitizers ready for free distribution, face masks for community workers and also the society. The resident staff got together and quickly put together packets of grocery and also food packets to be delivered to those who needed succour in these times.

As a part of REVA's contribution to the society at large REVA resident staff and students during these turbulent times, with adequate safety measures ensured that the society was benefitted by our initiatives be it in supplying masks with easily available materials, which were washable, manufacturing sanitizers and also putting together a ventilator for human support.

Figure 1.31: Combating COVID

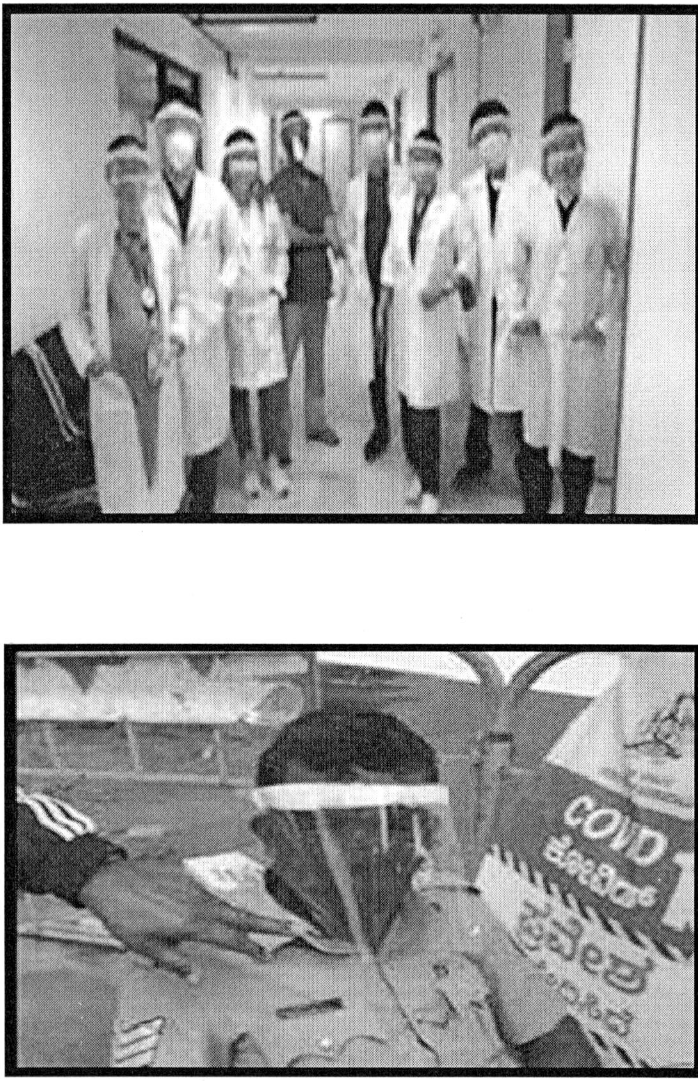

Figure 1.32: Outreach and Support

1.13.1 Community Support: REVA University supports social causes through and through as a part of University Social Responsibility. The reach is first made to the community close by and since the University works with some socially impacting bodies–like the BBMP, the first reach was made to BBMP Office. The dispenser was of need to such an office due to its service to the society during these times.

REVA University has reached out to the public to provide essential food services in form of daily food packets to the needy. Over 1,40,000 food packets have been distributed already from REVA Hostel Kitchen as a wonderful gesture from our Chancellor Dr P Shyama Raju and the REVA Family.

National Cadet Corps (NCC) members of REVA University have been a vital part of providing awareness to the people with the importance of lockdown, social distancing and providing the citizens with the do's and don'ts during the COVID-19 crisis. This mass campaign has helped provide valuable information to help the people stay safe and secure during these troubled times.

Figure 1.33: Auto Hand Sanitizer

REVA believes in extending support to the needy and during times of distress like this, one REVA family came forward and donated immensely to the welfare of the citizens by contributing in kind and cash.

Figure 1.34: Auto Hand Sanitizer

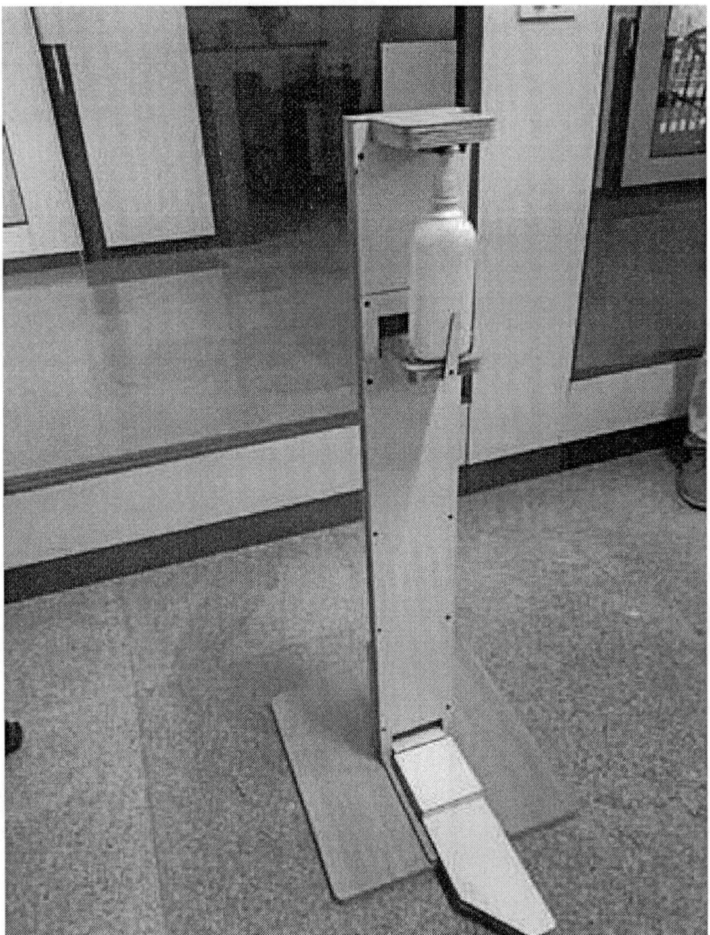

1.14 Concluding Notes

With this successful intervention and quick adaptability of the team at REVA, the first phase which included conclusion of exams and also computation of results went on successfully. Armed with all these efforts and strategies in place REVA was invited by QS to participate in its First batch E-LEAD Certification Survey were REVA was listed amongst pioneer Universities in the country and was given the E-LEAD recognition certificate on the 14th May, 2020 virtually by Shri. Ramesh Pokhriyal, Hon'ble Union Minister, HRD and Dr. Pankaj Mittal, AIU.

Figure 1.35: E-LEAD Certificate

All at REVA realized that Universities have a critical role to play in preparing young minds to go on and as part of the New Normal it was important the University thought of creating alternate sustainable plans. The next section focusses on the other key focus areas at the campus which included getting the campus ready, developing curricula and pedagogies oriented towards the new needs of the situation and working towards an ecosystem that would enable students come back to campus safe and secure.

2

Reset: Campus Opening Plan

2.1 Moving Forward: The New Normal

Once the lockdown was lifted, it was important that the entire University garnered support and ensured that plans were in place for the new beginnings. Since the staff were the first to come back it was important that the campus was ready in all aspects. The focus was only on keeping the campus ready to ensure that minimal staff and all essential services were in place. The campus took a new definition and new existence as measures were strategically planned to get back people to the campus without disrupting the ecosystem that was already safe and secure.

It was decided that we divide the reopening phase keeping in mind many factors and in alignment with Government directives for transition. In the meantime, REVA needed to develop, revisit some of the existing practices and guidelines. Our operation plans required revisit and focus was on preparedness of the campus. Our mitigation strategies were worked on and you would have read in the first section of this book the various strategies that we had already set in place right from sanitizers to scanners to fumigation to social distancing measures in campus. What we had to focus on next was to develop individual school wise transition plans, alternative teaching-learning plans and plan for all stakeholders, which included but were not limited to:

1. Moderate restrictions of staffing
2. Moderate hours of operation for students
3. Moderate hours of operation of services
4. Protocols to be implemented for students and staff, bearing in mind health and safety and security of all
5. Rescheduled events and travel restrictions

6. Workplace directives.
7. Hostel safety measures.

2.2 Campus Access

Campus re-opening to all employees was done in a phased manner. Non-employees were not entertained in the campus. Expectations were set for all employees to follow the strict guidelines as listed earlier. These security measures enabled us bounce back to work and gradually open the campus for the public. Social distancing protocol measures will be strictly followed going forward and administrators will have zero tolerance implementation of these guidelines. Work spaces reallocation was done and all Directors were made responsible for the rearrangement of work spaces, increased distances between work spaces, signage and instructions for all team members.

Acclimatizing the faculty to the new normal (Figure 2.1) was very important and it began with a communique on post lockdown preventive measures and guidelines shared with all faculty members.

Figure 2.1: Post Lockdown Communique

post lockdown precaution

Chancellor Office
Fri 5/1/2020 9:03 PM
To: All; All 1
Cc: Dr. P Shyamaraju; Umesh Raju; Tanisha Raju; Dr. Dhananjaya M

postlockdownmeasures.pdf

Dear REVA family

Greetings!

As mentioned during Chinthan today, I want you to go through all the guidelines that has been listed in the attachment and follow this carefully so that we take up prudent measures and prevent the spread of the virus.

Warm Regards,

Dr P Shyama Raju
Chancellor
Off: 080 46966966

Figure 2.1: Post Lockdown Communique

REVA UNIVERSITY

POST LOCKDOWN PRECAUTIONS TO BE FOLLOWED

After a long lockdown which was unexpected we at REVA are now at a stage where we are planning step by step execution of Post COVID measures and of how to get back to our daily routine one step at a time. Of course, we cannot hurry ourselves and therefore during these days of lockdown, through all our online meetings we have been discussing how to plan the next steps and ensure there is safety to life. COVID-19 has taught us many lessons and one great lesson it has taught us is patience and tolerance towards Nature. As we all know, CO stands for Corona, VI stands for Virus and D stands for Disease...so it is a Virus Disease which if not controlled can destroy life. Because it is a Disease, the Government declared lock down and seal down of some places. Because it is a Virus, we need to be careful for if not controlled it can spread. Protecting ourselves and protecting our students is important for us.

At REVA, I am happy each of you as a teacher cooperated very well with the online teaching and support. All our hostel students reached their homes safely and we took the right decisions at the right time. Our campus has been maintained safe till date, we need to continue to sustain these safety measures. Our students, their parents and yes most of us are also scared. It may be because some of us are at an age which is under risk apart from the fact that some of us have health problems and so may be at risk. It is our responsibility to ensure our safety and also care for the students. The first fear of students are their exams, their future and also what will happen next year. We need to take care of their anxieties and therefore mentoring is important.

Back at campus we need to plan and follow all guidelines as listed below:

2.3 Guidelines Shared with the Faculty:

- If unwell or sick, do not report to work, inform the HR and inform the Director.
- Wearing own washable and sanitized masks to work is a must.
- Carrying a sanitizer in the pocket, develop this as a habit like carrying a wallet or a purse.
- Wash hands regularly, but be careful not to waste water.
- When entering the campus, follow the rules set, use the sanitizer, wait patiently for the thermal scan to be done.
- In the campus a systematic entry to the walkway, to the driveway and marking is done on the ground and on the common floors apart from marking on the parapet for sitting.
- Social distancing inside the campus is a must and is non-negotiable.
- Do not get into groups.
- Avoid walking around the campus unnecessarily.
- Do not go home and go visiting friends, get into groups or visit markets and any other sensitive place.
- Do not attend any gatherings or social meetings.
- Your staff room and work places are disinfected, maintain the same.
- Avoid using the lifts.
- Do not switch on the AC but use the windows generously.
- Lunch should be brought from home along with your safe drinking water.
- Avoid sitting in groups for lunch.
- Do not use others cups, glass, boxes, plates to eat.
- Do not use others stationery.
- Keep the door handles and other surfaces used frequently sanitized and clean.
- We have staggered your reporting dates, follow the time table set, please do not negotiate on guidelines.

- In the staff room keep your chairs apart and work with your masks on.
- Keep your computers sanitized, mobile phones sanitized.
- Get used to limited communication and avoid gossip over phone.
- Understand facts and figures and please do not discuss fake news.
- Do not terrify people or tease each other or create any unpleasantness for anybody.
- Unwanted use of phone is not a healthy practice.
- Focus on online strategies for teaching and other activities as per directives given.
- Use the toilets and maintain them clean.
- Do not cough or sneeze without covering your mouth.
- Avoid touching your face.
- Lady faculty should avoid bringing leather bags.
- Sanitizers are placed everywhere in the campus.
- Do not litter anywhere.
- Sanitize your ID cards regularly.
- Wear fresh clothes to work and ensure your entire team does it.
- Travel safe to work, practice social distancing even in your own cars.
- Compliance with Government rules and guidelines given is a must.
- Please use social media sensibly.
- Your office staff, your attenders and other staff are your responsibility, ensure they are guided from time to time and with sensitivity.
- More than anything, remember this is your life and you have to be responsible for your life.
- If there is health, there is wealth and value of life is important.

Outside of campus activities and gathering in common areas, use of elevators and using others equipment without care, using others desks, cubicles and phones in the campus have been prohibited. All in-person meetings have been limited to 3 to 5 persons and with social distancing or else MS Office Teams meetings are conducted. Each School Director is expected to establish protocols for monitoring symptoms of students, scheduling activities, classroom movement, social distancing, seating, alternate days of classes and monitoring movement in the campus. For the commencement of the classes it was decided to create student groups so that it is easier to monitor students by the mentors. Classroom seating was planned to have good air flow and students seating in classrooms have been sketched in detail with good ventilation measures.

It was unanimously decided that at all the meetings and deliberations held at REVA, we will continue to use virtual platforms like MS Teams to efficiently conduct all the online sessions for students if the permission to start the sessions offline is not lifted. Faculty at REVA will continue to remotely connect with all the learners and conduct interactive classes as per the scheduled sessions for the new semester. MS Teams with its various integrated tools, like, fully integrated Office 365, conversational channels, Onedrive, Sharepoint, whiteboard, planners will be used extensively not just for the sessions, but also for connecting with fellow learners outside the formal sessions bringing the real joy of collaborative efforts and teamwork.

The session plans of various courses have been customized and reset to meet the learner needs and the learning online will continue to be seamless and a joy to all learners with conscious efforts to ensure a normal classroom environment is created including labs, studios and theory sessions without diluting the quality of academic delivery.

2.4 For Students

Campus will be open to students as and when there are Government directives for reopening. Social distancing measures for students will also remain the same. Students will have to come in wearing face shields or face masks and if disposable masks are used, then the masks have to be disposed outside the campus and in a closed bin only.

While in the campus, students will wear the masks at all times within buildings and in common areas including the library and labs and workshops. The University will purchase cloth masks and these masks will be made available for students just in case they forget the face cover or there is any damage of the mask that they have been wearing. The detailed face mask guidelines which needs to be referred to by all students are listed below.

2.5 Guidelines for Wearing Face Masks

1. It is recommended for students to wear cloth face masks when they are in public spaces.
2. It is mandatory to wear face masks to the campus every day.
3. Wearing of face masks as you walk around the campus is must.
4. Cloth face covering will help us to prevent from spreading the virus in the campus.
5. Do not wear wet face masks, for it will make difficult to breath.
6. Dispose the face mask only in the assigned bins.
7. Do not leave your face mask unattended.
8. Reuseable face mask should be cleaned and disinfected after each use.
9. As you remove the mask pull it away from the face.

It is important that all students go through the campus guidelines which is on the website and also ensure daily temperature screenings are done. Once inside the campus, the gates will be open only for exit and at periodic and set timings and exit and entry is as per the controlled guidelines of the security.

If there is fever detected, then the student will be asked to leave the campus till there is a supporting medical document of fitness and this is non-negotiable. Any updates or changes to the protocol will be done as and when required and posted on the University website. Testing of all students, faculty and staff who return to campus is mandatory.

A medical certificate as required from each student and staff member has to be submitted to the reporting authority at the main gate (Figure 2.2).

Figure 2.2: Medical Certificate

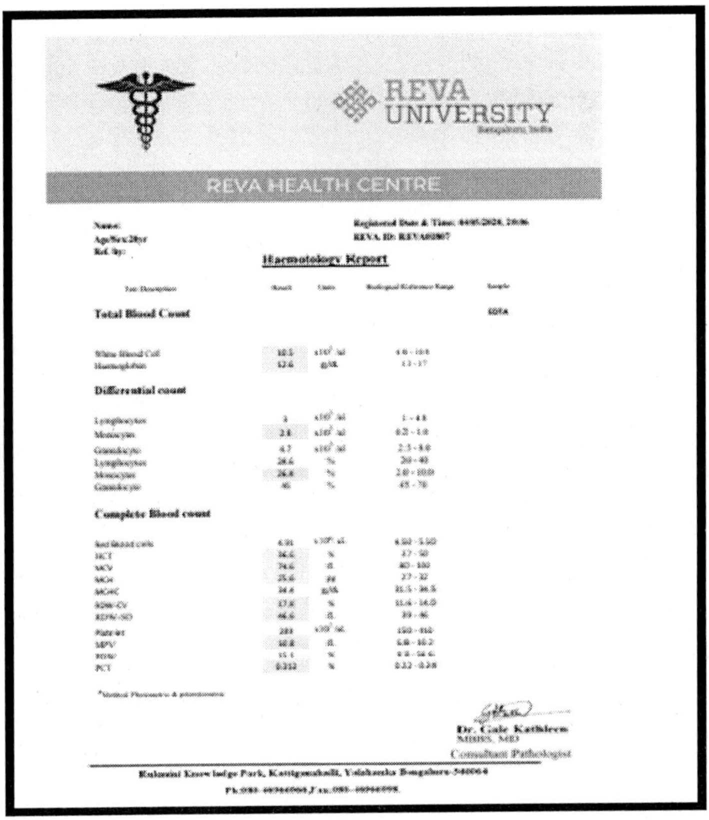
REVA UNIVERSITY

REVA HEALTH CENTRE

Haematology Report

Total Blood Count

Differential count

Complete Blood count

Dr. Gale Kathleen

Consultant Pathologist

Campus opening will be in a phased manner and with limited numbers and alternate days of classes as scheduled by the individual schools. Faculty will trace student movements and activities.

Schools will offer a mix of online and in-person classes. Lunch hours and tea breaks will be staggered and students will have to adopt to the shifts as scheduled. Normal operations will resume only once vaccine or treatment is available and as per Government directives.

2.6 Sample of Guidelines for Students

1. Students are expected to carry sanitizers, wear masks and gloves.
2. Students are expected to use cloth bags to carry books, which can be washed regularly.
3. Kindly produce the CBC report before reporting to the University to your respective mentors.
4. Students are hereby instructed to carry snack, lunch and drinking water to the University.
5. Students who are reporting to the University should also ensure that if they have any travel history then they are expected to quarantine themselves for 14 days.
6. Students residing in Red Zone or Containment Zones should give proper details to their respective Mentors.
7. Students are expected to follow all the precautionary measures undertaken by the University and cooperate with the security personnel and staff members who are involved in ensuring safety and health of students and staff.
8. University will take responsibility in ensuring the safety and health of students and staff within the University Premises.
9. Students and Staff members commuting in University Transport should ensure that they cooperate with the Transport staff and should compulsorily maintain physical distance inside the bus and follow all rules laid down thereby.

10. Students and staff should also cooperate in maintaining hygiene and cleanliness in restrooms and classrooms.
11. Students who would like to use the restroom will be made to stand in queue in the corridors where marking will be done. They will have to carry the sanitizers along with them.
12. 40 students seated in a class room will be guided to restrooms on one end and next 40 students seated will be guided to restrooms which are on the other side. Meanwhile as we divert the students to use the other rest room on the other side, the house keeping staff will be instructed to clean the restroom. So alternatively the restrooms will be used.
13. Students will have to maintain 75% minimum attendance to take up all tests and examinations of the University. Attendance will be marked for both online and offline classes and the same will be recorded in manual attendance registers and also the ERP at the end of every class and day.
14. Every student will be allotted a Mentor and the mentor will be responsible to keep in touch with their mentees, parents/guardians and give them complete details pertaining to academics and other activities of their mentees.

2.7 Housekeeping Protocols

Cleaning of the campus as per the routine guidelines will be done and best practices have been implemented to keep the campus safe and hygienic for all. Routine cleaning, disinfecting of work surfaces and areas like the restrooms, offices and workstations will be done. This being the case, crowding and standing in the reception area is restricted, grouping in open spaces is restricted, seating on the parapet is as per the marking, walking into the building is as per the marking, crowding in the stationery centre, library, lab entry and gym and other approved areas and activities will be under surveillance and each School has developed its own guidelines in keeping with the general guidelines.

Figure 2.3: PPE Kits Prepared

2.8 Post-COVID Lockdown World at the Hostels

Considering COVID-19 and its impact across the world, REVA has defined a new operating model to manage the hostels and resident staff and assure parents of the safety of their wards while at campus. Initiatives that have been taken up include: Regular sanitization and deep cleaning of zones where staff and their families. Mandatory use of protective equipment by all staff is monitored. Since the hostels have kitchens of their own, contactless food delivery and dining by strict adherence to best-in-class SOPs is shared with all.

Security is briefed on daily thermal monitoring at entry/exit points of residences. In order to minimize service disruptions to the hostels, bulk securing of non-perishables and proactive earmarking of supplies with supplier is done. Apart from this, since our Hostels are run by the University office and admin, we have ensured utmost hygiene and sanitisation measures are taken into account. Our kitchen staff have been trained to follow strict protocols on hygiene, sanitisation and usage of personal protective equipment. Occupancy arrangement were reworked on so as to avoid too many dorms.

During the lock down the hostel team was quick to revisit the hostel operations and come up with measures to ensure that students are safe once they are back in campus. Accordingly room allocation plans were reworked and every single team member was addressed. Since the University has almost 30% of the students residing in these residences, the hostel readiness was of utmost importance.

Accordingly, the following measures were taken up:

1. Parents and students already residing in the hostels were written to and communication was ongoing.
2. It was understood that parents preferred their wards to stay in the hostel which was safer rather than travel.
3. Students who were applying from remote areas and other states could virtually see the hostels through the website.
4. Hostel reservations also could be done online. This saved the parent the worry about blocking residences.
5. This is the time for students to fill in online forms, seek guidance from wardens when they are at home and ensure there is admission continuity.
6. Information about bank tie ups for fee payments and easy access to all documents that is required for hostel payments was shared.
7. Sanitisation of the entire hostel block has been taken care of.

8. Personal supervision will be done for all hostel rooms for cleanliness.
9. Dedicated faculty for close monitoring.
10. Enforcing hygiene and monitored care in hostels and the campus.
11. Caution to avoid public gatherings and especially during festive time.
12. Caution to avoid outside food.
13. Increased placing of hand sanitizers in campus and strategic locations.
14. Housekeeping training is ongoing.
15. Increased cleaning levels is ongoing.
16. Equipped medical centre.
17. Medical hospitals for emergency care and labs.
18. Alert food delivery.
19. Promoting safe travel.
20. Maintaining high personal hygiene.
21. Nutritious and balanced meal.

2.9 Re-engineered Academic experience

We will continue to deliver a rigorous and innovative academic experience to all our students. We will continue with our practices of setting highest academic standards and offer a blend of high-impact learning in person and a higher-impact learning experience remotely if necessary. We will continue to invest in our unique career-readiness plans and programs for enhancing employability will continue.

2.9.1 The Blended Mode: Our focus will be on the blended system of learning to ensure there is no disruption in the teaching-learning process of the students. REVA will hold lectures online for the students till there is clearance for reopening of the campus. Once the campus reopens we will adopt a combination of face to face and online instruction. Some courses will have more content than the others but that will not deter the University from exploring newer methods to deliver the content as a close match to classroom learning.

While we hope that we will be able to deliver face-to-face teaching soon, the studies of students will go online and transition to on-campus study will be done gradually as and when circumstances allow. Online learning is a big challenge to both students and teachers as there is a sudden shift to online learning. Online learning involves a different set of skills and it is the responsibility of every Director along with IQAC to ensure that faculty guidelines for online teaching are adhered to and followed scrupulously. All our learning resources will have to be planned in such a manner that students can access their content from remote parts of the country and also content accessibility needs to be there on all devices. The blended classroom instructors are trained in use of technology and there has been identified a need to organize and deliver material accordingly which will be done at the earliest. There is a need to realize that the shift of online teaching has transferred a lot of responsibility of learning to the students. This means that the teachers have to sustain class interest and material delivery will need a lot more effort and make student active participants in this process.

We will need to ensure that these classes are far more effective by bringing in collaborative learning online, group assignments. It is important that the course handout is shared with all the learners well in advance and using the formal platform and as per the course format shared. We need to plan which are the topics that will go online as per the detailed syllabus for the semester...begin with easier topics based on need analysis, adaptation of the content and materials. Also we will need to bear in mind the pedagogy to be employed, the course requirement, the different learning styles of students and also their preferences. Along with this we will have to use as many types of video/audio content as possible. Keeping in mind that online teaching requires self-paced learning faculty should ensure that adequate gap in between the sessions is given apart from ensuring that faculty should not continue with lecture led sessions for long hours. Faculty need to specifically explain rules in one session which sets expectations between the faculty and the student. Faculty have to always conduct a live session for discussion and keep timed and paced assessments, collaborative work with each other. All teachers have to set the practice of taking feedback of the courses as per the timelines given and as per the template offered by the University. At this stage assignments given should be engaging for the student and with minimal technical requirement. The faculty needs to explain the assignment as clearly as possible before giving out the assignment. It is crucial that faculty provide timely feedback to students as well during mentoring sessions and use as many life-examples as possible while teaching apart from motivating the students. Very important that faculty spend time for question and answer sessions and study the detailed process put in place for the teacher by the University.

2.9.2 Planning Online Assignments: For planning online assignments, faculty are given guidelines by each school which range from planning assignments well ahead of time to feedback. All assignments during this time need thorough discussion with students. Expectation setting becomes important. It is important during these times that the rubrics are explained to students before the grading of assignments. Along with the rubrics the faculty must drop the assignment on LMS well in advance with timelines for submission. Smaller details like the format for submission to evaluation timeframe can add value. Apart from this, discussion and feedback on performance will add that personal touch.

2.9.3 E-Content Guidelines: Academic Planning: The Academic Directors were the quickest to put their plans in place to face all kinds of situations that come up with the post COVID new world. The team got together to prepare and look at various plans that the University as a whole should engage in apart from preparing model plans for each School.

2.10 Steps followed while planning the Academic Deliverables Post-COVID

Step 0: Aligning to the academic calendar
Step 1: Included trifurcating the plan into 3 groups
Step 2: Split of semesters and freeze on commencement dates
Step 3: Demographic study
Step 4: Understanding the infrastructure support
Step 5: Determining the classroom occupancy
Step 6: Time-table planning
Step 7: Curriculum planning
Step 8: Planning of units under each subject
Step 9: Workload allocation
Step 10: Checklist

A sample structure for an Engineering School (School of Architecture) included the following steps.

Step 0: Academic Calendar

Figure 2.4: Rescheduled Classes

CALENDAR OF EVENTS (JULY' 2020 - DECEMBER' 2020)

PROPOSED SCHEDULE OF TESTS/EXAMINATIONS FOR ENGINEERING PROGRAMS

FINAL COPY

Sl. No.	Programs	Date of Re-Opening	Schedule							Vacation	Commencement of next semester
			IA 1	Results	IA 2	Results	Practical / Project Exams	Semester End Exams	Results		
1	B. Tech - III, V, VII, Sem B.Arch - III, V, VII, IX Sem	27-Jul-2020	07-Sep-2020 to 10-Sep-2020	18-Sep-2020	21-Oct-2020 to 24-Oct-2020	2-Nov-2020	30-Nov-2020 to 12-Dec-2020	14-Dec-2020 to 30-Dec-2020	7-Jan-2021	31-Dec-2020 to 09-Jan-2021	11-Jan-2021
3	M.Tech - III Sem	27-Jul-2020	07-Sep-2020 to 10-Sep-2020	18-Sep-2020	21-Oct-2020 to 24-Oct-2020	2-Nov-2020	30-Nov-2020 to 12-Dec-2020	14-Dec-2020 to 30-Dec-2020	7-Jan-2021	31-Dec-2020 to 09-Jan-2021	11-Jan-2021

Tentative Date of commencement	Programs
17-Aug-20	1st Semester - UG programs (Non-Engineering)
2-Sep-20	1st Semester - UG programs (Engineering)
2-Sep-20	1st Semester - PG programs (Non-Engineering)
21-Sep-20	1st Semester - M.Tech, MBA, MCA

Figure 2.4: The New Normal @ School of Architecture

Step 1: Included Trifurcating the Plan into 3 Groups

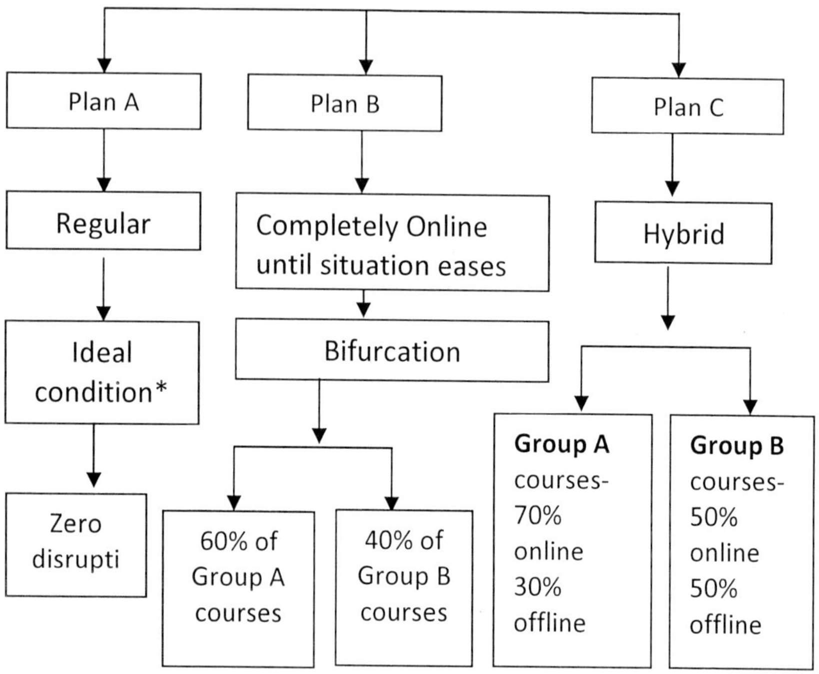

Plan A invariably forms the most preferred situation on Earth, where we pray the world is healed and normalcy prevails. However, that being a distant possibility and based on hope and prayers alone, Plan B and C is where the focus lay.

Plan B would encompass a lot more detailing since students would stay home and all courses would be delivered online only. The School preferred 60% of the time being devoted to online courses and 40% of the time to be allocated to offline sessions or alternate modes of sessions as this School needed a lot more focus on studio courses and courses that need hands-on learning.

Plan C on the other hand would entail students attending lecture sessions at campus to begin with on alternate days and with a preference for 3 days in a week.

Further, it was planned that students from alternate semesters would be in campus on any given day. Since all courses have an online and offline component, the School divided this further into:

1. Group A courses: 70% online; 30% offline (bearing in mind the need for hands on support and specific plans to be made further to compensate this learning support).
2. Group B courses: 50% online, 50% offline.

Timetable was accordingly customized to stagger break timings for students.

Step 2: Split of Semesters and Freeze on Commencement Dates: The Academic calendar was frozen for the year ahead, so that there was a realistic conclusion drawn on the possible number of working days and also an insight into where does the School squeeze time to balance the deliverables without compromising on quality.

Since the new admits would come in later, the Schools decided to focus on the higher semesters on priority (Figure 2.5).

Step 3: Demographic Study: Using the ERP and also a quick survey done with parents, the School sought clarity on the demographics of its student population.

This was important to arrive at the number of students and the number of classrooms requirement based on the new norms of social distancing and also limited movement within the classrooms and all other spaces within the building.

The demographic study enabled the school to understand how many students could attend campus classes on alternate days and how many students have to be supported with online classes (Figure 2.6).

Figure 2.5:
Step 2: Split of Semesters and Freeze on Commencement Dates

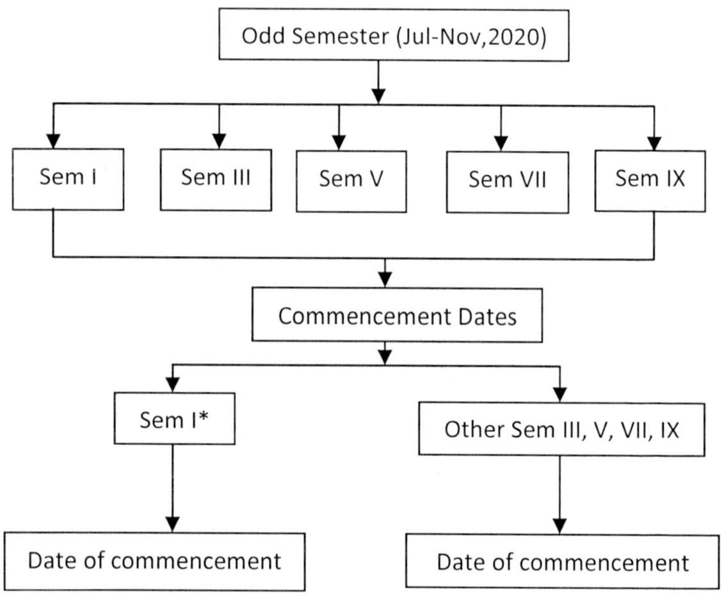

* Subject to Government guidelines

Figure 2.6:
Step 3: Demographic Study

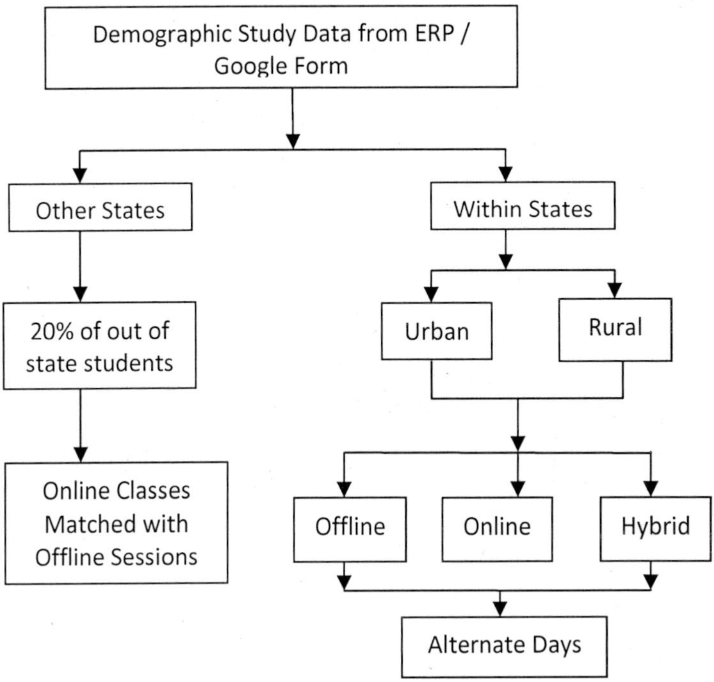

Step 4: Understanding the Infrastructure Support: At REVA with the vision being Digital REVA, most of the classes have ICT support. The only requirement was to ensure that ICT support in labs and studios was provided for. This was important because most of the Engineering classes are studio and lab dependent. School Directors were quick to measure and indent the number of classrooms required for ICT support. Wherever acoustic treatment classrooms were required, arrangements were made for the same (Figure 2.7).

Figure 2.7:
Step 4: Understanding the Infrastructure Support

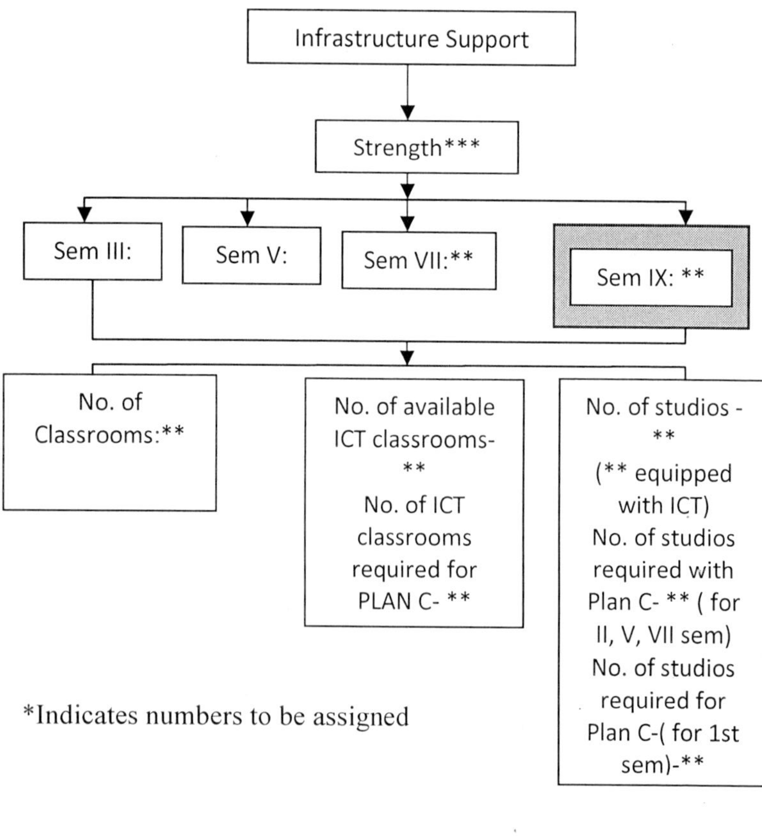

*Indicates numbers to be assigned

Step 5: Determining the Classroom Occupancy: Involved determining the classroom occupancy for all semesters based on the subject combinations and the strength of the class. This meant seating could be planned in accordance with the determined occupancy. This also enabled the next step of determining the time table for alternate days and semesters.

Figure 2.8

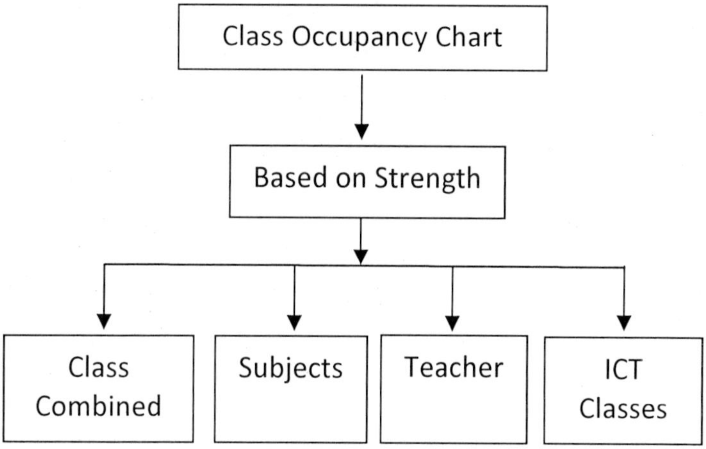

Step 6: Time Table Planning: The next step was to study the core subjects to be offered both online and offline. Accordingly, the time table had to be framed bearing in mind group A courses, group B courses and also keeping in mind the class strength and the classrooms. Slots were to be given for one to one extra discussions with faculty members for online students. Slots for Peer learning sessions for students who went online and offline to discuss the learnings had to be provisioned for. Customized time tables for certain semesters had to be planned. Apart from that mentoring sessions had to be incorporated. The class duration was reduced for some subjects.

Step 7: Curriculum Planning: Along side the time table planning, faculty geared up for session planning to support the hybrid system. Pedagogy was revisited to ensure that classes were interesting and sustaining. Special guidelines were drawn up for electives which included special lectures by external experts through online mode for supplementary learning. Flipped classroom and collaborative learning modules had to be included for all elective courses (Figure 2.9).

Figure 2.9:
Step 7: Curriculum Planning

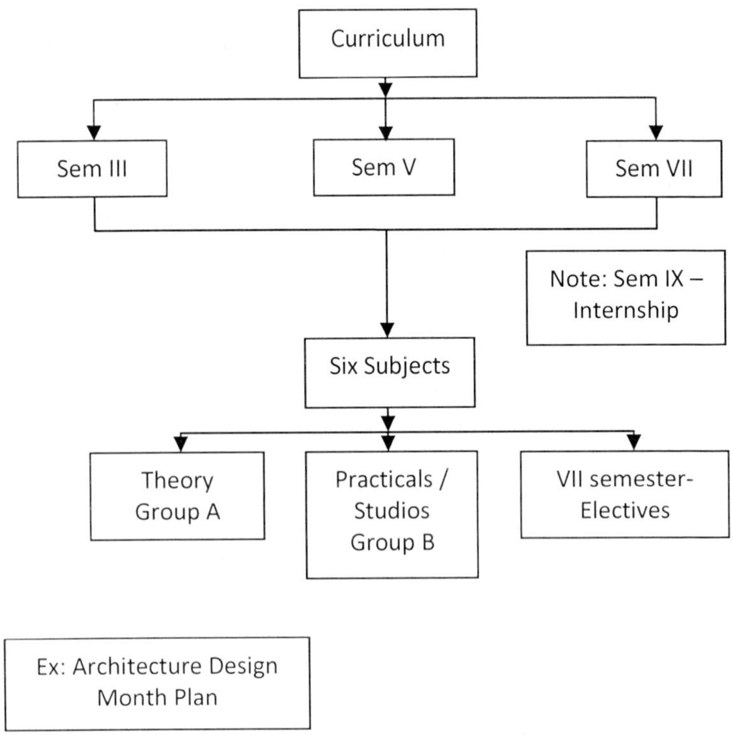

Step 8: Planning of Units under each Subject: Each school decided to revisit the number of units under each subjects so that units were selected based on online and offline classes (Figure 2.10).

- **Group A courses** were planned in a such a manner that self study/research component comes towards Units 3 and 4 once basic learning and introduction to concepts is completed in Unit 1 and 2.
- **Group B courses:** Unit wise progression was planned keeping in mind incremental learning. Basic concepts were introduced in Unit 1 and 2. Complex topics were planned to be taken up in Units 3 and 4.
- **Electives:** Basic concepts were planned to be introduced in Units 1 and 2.

Figure 2.10

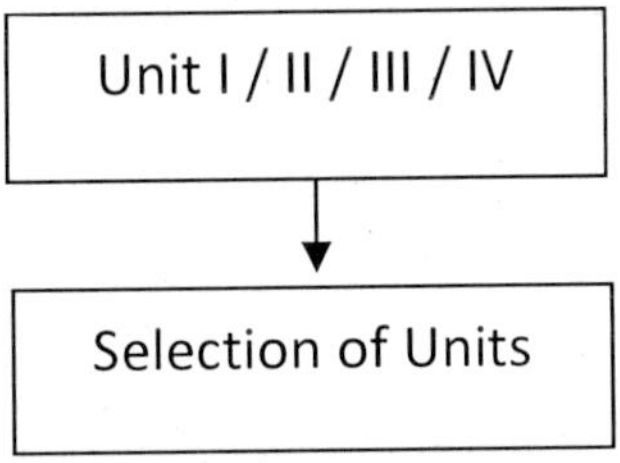

Step 9: Workload Allocation: Workload Allocation was revisited since each section would be split according to the strength into different sections.

Plans were put in place to ensure that one faculty's lectures and sessions were beamed to all the other sections. This would also accommodate all the online classes.

Step 10: Checklist: A checklist was drawn up to capture all the various pedagogical tools and support for each course as below (Figure 2.11).

Figure 2.11

	Lectures	Lectures+ PPT	Video link	Assign-ments
Unit 1 Sub-topic 1 Sub-topic 2 Sub-topic 3 Sub-topic 4				
Unit 2 Sub-topic 1 Sub-topic 2 Sub-topic 3 Sub-topic 4				

	Discussions/ reviews	Flipped classroom	Quiz
Unit 1 Sub-topic 1 Sub-topic 2 Sub-topic 3 Sub-topic 4			
Unit 2 Sub-topic 1 Sub-topic 2 Sub-topic 3 Sub-topic 4			

2.11 A Sample Structure for a Non-Engineering School (School of Commerce and Management Studies)

The beginning for the schools was to ensure that the communication with parents is ongoing and they are kept informed about all the plans in progress and those that are to be implemented stage wise.

The initial steps would be to communicate with the parents about the alternate plans that the School has put in place for the new semester. This includes a letter that would go from the Director to the parents–a sample of which is as below.

2.12 Post-COVID Commencement of Academic Session: A New Norm: Message from the School Director

Amidst uncertainties and many ups and downs that each one of us faced in the last few months, I must firstly appreciate and thank all parents, guardians and students for being supportive and extending your cooperation in enabling us to continue teaching and learning even during the toughest time. Due to the sudden outbreak of CORONA, every sector is affected in one way or the other, but thanks to technology we have stayed connected with our students and parents. At REVA, we always believe very positively that nothing can stop us from staying connected with our students academically and emotionally.

I strongly believe that educating the child is the responsibility of every parent, university, teacher and also students. Learning should not stop come what may. In this regard every single effort has been put in by the University and respective school to ensure that academic and emotional well-being of students is taken care. It is important now, that, just as in the last few months that you supported us, the same support and cooperation would be extended from all stake holders.

I understand as parents you would be really worried for your wards and to give you assurance and to prepare you to take up the next academic session with confidence all preparations are done at the University campus. Post-COVID-19 as we all agree the life is not going to be the same for all of us wherever we are. It is important that we learn to be positive, take all necessary precautionary measures and also most importantly we need to develop our immunity levels to fight against the virus.

As we ensure this, we also need to reaffirm ourselves that learning should continue, the classes for higher semester UG (3rd and 5th semesters) and PG (3rd semester) will be commencing in the month of July, initially with online classes and later on once the situation is safe to start based on the directives of the state Government and other statutory bodies; the classes would commence offline too with staggered working days.

The new norm would be new seating matrix for students, staggered classes, revisited hostel and library rules, limited mobility of hostel students outside campus to reduce the health risk. Students will have to go through the screening process stringently.

We also hope and expect that all parents and guardians will cooperate with us in avoiding weekend travel of your ward residing in hostel.

Standard operating procedures are prepared to ensure that students maintain social and physical distancing in the campus, classrooms, labs, library and transport, playgrounds and so on. Separate lanes for entry and exit of students is planned and the route map is drawn and sign boards are put up. Every block will be following staggered entry and exit timings and multiple entry and exits are identified too.

All parents will be marked a complete set of dossier, which will clearly indicate the preparations made by the University to start the academic session. This dossier is prepared to ensure the safety of students and staff and we urge all parents to cooperate and trust our efforts.

We assure you that we will not let you down. I would also like to bring to your notice that post-COVID-19 the new rules and procedures have to be strictly followed and adhered by all students. As a University we would also like to assure all parents that we will conduct and organise awareness programs pertaining to COVID-19 and we will ensure that our students are emotionally and mentally strong.

Join hands as we begin this new journey with blended teaching and learning, learning with social and physical distancing as we course through this journey together.

Teaching-Learning

Teaching and learning is a process that needs strategic initiatives and planning to be implanted to handle the challenges post by the pandemic to the academic process. Every challenge comes with an opportunity and this problem of COVID-19 has also opened up new opportunities in the academic sector.

Many see this situation as a threat but I would like to see it positively and take it as an opportunity to adopt new things in the process of teaching and learning. With my experience in the field of education I have often experienced that bringing change in academics is really difficult and also changing the mindset of people involved in academics is time consuming process, but once they are convinced and committed they will ensure that they take the idea to the logical end. But what is the greatest challenge is taking that first step towards change.

In academics, strong conviction, determination and dedication is required. Students join universities, educational institutes and Schools to get classroom experience, interact with faculty, campus experience and other facilities. Now the argument is whether all this can be ensured to students through remote learning. Let me confidently tell you that in the prevailing situation many new ideas, approaches and techniques have been explored by faculty to make their teaching process effective. Education is going to be complex and varied as a University catering to the needs of the higher education. It is important for us to explore and plan new initiatives at macro, micro and operational level.

Before we get into the argument of conventional teaching learning v/s remote teaching learning, we must first understand the purpose of education. Educational institutions and Universities are not to be considered as Machineries to produce graduates in mass numbers but instead we should rather focus on how to deliver and create value for our stakeholders. The concept of education is going to change in days to come.

Education is not the only way that we can build their future, we need to adopt realistic approach in all that we do in academics.

Making students 'Person of Utility' is important. In this regard, we should focus on increasing and emphasizing the student experience.

Future is going to technology enabled teaching-learning process. It is better to understand the future needs not only from the pandemic point of view but also because it is the need of the hour. Each one of us involved in the teaching and learning process should learn to embrace change and get accustomed to the new norm.

Today, whether it is a parent or a student they come with set of expectations. From the parent perspective they want value for money and from the student point of view he/she needs good academic experience and exposure with no compromise in quality.

As teachers and facilitators it is very important for each one of you to understand what is expected only then you will be able to deliver your academic offerings effectively. Usually, this is where the gap exists, the gap exists between expectation and actual delivery.

Gaps in Academics = Expectation from Stakeholders – Actual Delivery

During this pandemic all faculty members across have adopted digital modes for delivery of the courses. Just adopting and delivering the courses through an online platform may not meet the expectations of the stakeholders. Instead we should try to give them an experience which is much more enduring than the conventional mode.

For this, today various resources and options are available for facilitators to deliver the course. Initially adoption challenges will be faced by both teachers and students but these challenges will in future become opportunities for growth and development.

This entire process needs an open mindset from teachers to learn adapt themselves to new changes. We are not trying to change the system of education nor you need to become an online teaching expert, instead we would like you to adopt a hybrid model that will enable us to retain the core values of the University and also enable us to establish a brand value for ourselves.

Faculty members need to enhance their capabilities and accept the new norm very gracefully. Teaching and learning would have otherwise also changed in the next 5 Years, change is not happening only because of the pandemic, but instead pandemic has preponed us to think on the changes that we would have seen 5 years later. But this situation we would have seen otherwise also.

Understanding the Needs

It is important for every teacher to understand how strong we are in offering courses virtually to students. How effectively can we engage our students? How to prepare Quality e-Content and how to ensure Quality evaluation and assessments virtually has to be explored.

For this systematic training is required for teachers to understand and learn how an e-Content could be developed. How to upload e-assignments, e-quizzes, projects, tests and assessments need some expert training to be given to empower teachers to handle the situation more confidently.

The virtual classroom culture is totally different from that of a conventional classroom culture, whether it is tools on techniques that you follow (or) the attendance management system the experience is going to be totally different. Change will also be experienced in the teacher-student relationship when you are virtually connected to them.

We all watch television every day at home, we also watch videos and use many apps in our mobile phones, when all these electronic gadgets connect us with various things and events happiness around the World, why can't we use electronic mode in teaching and learning to connect with our target audience for academics is a thought that I would like to throw light upon.

We should thank technology for keeping us connected in these difficult times rather than debating and arguing as to why we should teach online?

Answer is very simple we cannot leave a question as a question we also should take accountability and responsibility because it is the future and career of child that is in our hands.

2.13 Sample Monthly Plan for Online Teaching-Learning

Plan from July 2020 to August 2020: In view of health and safety of students the classes initially will resume using MS teams–TET–Technology Enabled teaching learning process will be adopted

Plan from September 2020 to Closure of the Semester: After reviewing the situation pertaining to COVID 19 and also based on the directives of the State Government and other statutory bodies the classes will resume OFFLINE, wherein students for the current odd semester will visit University two days a week and rest of the sessions will be TET.

2.14 Wireframe of Classes for School of Commerce and Management Studies: A Sample

First semester UG classes will be held on Mondays and Tuesdays as per timings below:

Timing	Session
8.30 am to 9.30 am	I Session
9.30 am to 10.30 am	II Session
10.30 am to 11.00 am	Bio break
11.00 am to 12.00 noon	III Session
12.00 noon to 1.00 pm	IV Session
1.00 pm to 1.45 pm	Lunch Break
1.45 pm to 2.45 pm	V Session
2.45 pm to 3.45 pm	VI Session
3.45 pm to 4.45 pm	VII Session

Allotment of Online and Offline Classes: Course-wise

Course	Offline Hours	Online Hours	Total Hours/ Week
Communicative English	2 hours	2 hours	4 hours
K/H/AE	2 hours	2 hours	4 hours
F.A/C	3 hours	1 hour	4 hours
MOB	2 hours	2 hours	4 hours
IFS	2 hours	2 hours	4 hours
Indian Economy	2 hours	2 hours	4 hours
ICHR	-------	2 hours	2 hours
SDC	-------	2 hours	30 contact hrs. for the course

Total Offline classes required (13 hours) to be conducted on Mondays and Tuesdays.
Monday – 8.30 am to 4.45 pm
Tuesday – 8.30 am to 3.45 pm
Total Online classes required (15 hours) to be conducted from Wednesday to Saturday.

Third semester classes for UG will be held on Wednesdays and Thursdays as per timings below:

Timing	Session
8.30 am to 9.30 am	I Session
9.30 am to 10.30 am	II Session
10.30 am to 11.00 am	Bio break
11.00 am to 12.00 noon	III Session
12.00 noon to 1.00 pm	IV Session
1.00 pm to 2.00 pm	V Session

2.15 Seating Arrangement for Offline Classes

1. 30 students will be allotted per classroom, all students will be allotted a unique seating numbers students are expected to sit in the same classroom every day and in the same bench only.
2. Seating Numbers are allotted on the basis of their SRN numbers in ascending order
   Example: B.Com (Industry Integrated) – CI001, CI002
   B.Com (Honours) – CH001, CH002 ....
   BBA (Industry Integrated) – BI001, BI002....
   BBA (Honours) – BH001, BH002....
   BBA (Entrepreneurship) – BE001, BE002...
   M.Com – MC001, MC002...
   MBA – MB001, MB002.....

Sample of seating arrangements as below:

REVA UNIVERSITY
Bengaluru, India

SCHOOL OF COMMERCE
III Semester B.Com (Industry Integrated)
Post COVID-19 - Students Seating Order

SL.No	SRN	Name of the Student	Seat No.
1	R18BC061	NIEGEL SAJI	CI-1
2	R18BC151	SUBBAIAH K G	CI-2
3	R18BC160	TEJAS K	CI-3
4	R18BC193	SHAIK SUHAIL	CI-4
5	R18BC195	SUMANTH KUMAR V	CI-5
6	R18BC203	SAURAV SINGH S	CI-6
7	R18BC220	MICHAEL BEVAN ALLAN A	CI-7
8	R19BC001	A KUSHAL	CI-8
9	R19BC002	ABHISHEK GOWDA M	CI-9
10	R19BC003	ACHINTHYA SUMUKH D	CI-10

2.16 REVA Academy for Corporate Excellence (RACE)

Based on the directives of Government, RACE may restart the regular sessions at the campus soon. However, a few of these learnings from our online learning experience are going to stay with us forever. During this time, more collaborative projects have started; many inter-disciplinary teams were formed; more interactive sessions and practice labs were conducted; many more webinars on newer topics were discussed. Lock-down has put RACE participants and the team on a truly fast track of learning, breaking all the old boundaries and setting new goals in facilitating learning and transforming careers.

3

Recovery Strategies for REVA: The New Normal

3.1 Mentoring

In the current scenario of this busy world, majority of the parents are busy and occupied in their jobs and other commitments and they have entrusted their wards responsibility be it academic, health or personal to teachers, who as MENTORS should take care of their mentees and prepare them to face the challenges of life positively, supportively and successfully too. In this context the MENTORS should essentially understand the trust laid down by the parents with regards to their wards on the mentors.

3.1.1 Insightful Mentoring: Insightful accurate and deep understanding of the process of advising, guiding or training a less experienced or less knowledgeable person.

3.1.2 Mentor as a Person: Mentor is a person who willingly dedicates time and efforts to build a strong and productive relationship with his mentees and who focuses on Positive outcomes in due course of time.

3.1.3 Mentoring as a Process: Mentoring is a voluntary activity, where in mentors need to keep in touch with their respective mentees and their parents on a regular basis. This process requires patience and effective convincing communication through which you will be able to build a strong and lasting impression amongst mentees.

3.2 Expectations from Teacher as a Mentor

Expectations to be listed as a mentor requires the following attributes

1. Inspire
2. Guide

3. Role model
4. Coach
5. Cheer
6. Counsel
7. Connect
8. Comfort
9. Listener
10. Advisor
11. Educator
12. Accessible
13. Approachable
14. Compassionate
15. Available
16. Fairness
17. Positive attitude
18. Orient
19. Constructive approach
20. Productive
21. Feedback
22. Encourage
23. Build Trust
24. Goal Oriented
25. Purposeful

3.3 Types of Mentoring

3.3.1 One-to-One Mentoring:

1. Direct interaction with mentee.
2. To discuss issues which are confidential and personal to mentee.
3. Can be adopted to avoid negative consequences on the mentee.
4. To make the mentee feel secured.
5. To enable the mentee to freely communicate.

3.3.2 Distance Mentoring:

1. During COVID 19 all of you adopted Distance mentoring when both mentor and mentee are in distance location.

2. To stay connected when they are unable to meet each other directly.
3. To ensure that no gap exists due to distance and location.
4. Ensures concern even when geographically the mentor and mentee are located in different places.
5. It helps to eliminate isolation and depression and creates sense of belongingness and involvement.

3.3.3 Group Mentoring:

1. Process of mentoring students in a group to develop team spirit.
2. It enables them to learn to share, adjust, accommodate and learn from one another.
3. Enables to support and uplift one another.
4. Inspire to take up challenges.
5. Enables to open up freely and communicate effectively.

3.3.4 Effective Mentoring:

1. Mentoring is an activity which needs to be done very passionately and NOT as a mere duty, just to document or create reports.
2. Mentoring should be OUTCOME based, and essentially the outcome should be positive and as per expectation.
3. Mentors should sit with the list of students allotted to them as mentees and categorize them into 3 categories.

Category 1: Students who are disciplined, academically and personally responsible and who do not require too much counselling, but they essentially need to be appreciated, cautioned to be consistent as far as their responsibilities and accountability is concerned. They need to be recognised and pushed to take additional certifications, credits and also guided to participate in competitions and events. Such students' parents also need to be appreciated by Mentors by sending them a message of appreciation for giving their children the right upbringing and guidance.

Category 2: Students who are in average category, who keep fluctuating in their attitude, behaviour and there is NO consistency found either in their academics or personal life.

Such students need little more attention than Category 1, they take your guidance follow that for some time and again forget it. For such students, frequency of mentoring is to be increased. Here, the role of their parents also plays a vital role, it is better you take their parents to confidence and put efforts along with their parents to motivate them and keep them focused in the right direction.

Category 3: Students in this category need counselling on a daily basis. Hand-holding of such students is very important. As mentors, let us be sympathetic towards students in this category. Their behaviours, attitudes and performance might be an outcome of their frustrations, upbringing, problems untold too. With such students, challenge is more and also it would drain out all our energy, this is where each mentor will need the support of other colleagues to handle such challenging students. Here, we might also require support of professional counsellor too, if need be.

We cannot have neutral and uniform approach in handling students.

1. Mentoring fails when you feel that it is an imposed activity and you just do it for sake doing it. Every teacher is a mentor, role of a teacher is NOT only to teach the subjects to students and get good results in it. Instead every teacher should give first priority in teaching the LESSONS OF LIFE to students which will make them better individuals.
2. Mentoring should NOT be done to record in the documents, even though as a system recording and documentation needs to be done, but the ultimate objective of the entire process should be to see a POSITIVE CHANGE in the child.
3. Mentoring if NOT done correctly, can misguide, mislead, confuse, and create negativity and hatred too. This is because of the wrong approach adopted by the MENTORS.
4. Mentors should always try to develop a strong network and relationship with their mentees and their parents. But

in this process you should not forget your limits and you should not become unprofessional too. Restrict your interactions only to discuss the progress and activities of your mentee pertaining to academics only.

5. Mentors should not discuss about the personal life of students which may not be appreciated by students nor their parents.
6. In case of hostel students you should act like their local guardian or parent and should take complete responsibility about their academics, health and safety.
7. As Mentors you should be able to be problem solvers, information givers and not as liaison.
8. Success or failure of your mentees is your own success or failure.
9. Number does not really matter when the relationship is strong between you and your mentees.
10. Earlier, class teachers were whole and soul of their class. Time has changed, facilities, software has developed and today lot of options are available. In this scenario the mentoring should be even better.
11. Mentors need to have a lot of patience when they handle students and parents.
12. Mentors duty is not merely conducting meetings, passing on information to students in whatsapp, sending messages in ERP and calling their parents. The role of mentor should be re- defined and to be thought beyond this scope.
13. Mentoring should be done to see concrete changes in the student. Students should be able to develop gratitude and thankfulness towards University, school and all teachers.
14. Approach of mentoring should be done in broad sense and not from a narrow perspective.
15. Results of your mentoring will be evidently seen in the behaviour and attitude of your mentees.
16. Results and outcome of mentoring should not be temporary it should be permanent only then your efforts are successful. If the student whom you have groomed

over the period of time becomes a better human being, then mentoring is successful.

17. Mentoring is self-initiated activity, which needs to be done without anybody's supervision or monitoring.

3.4 Process of Mentoring

1. Know yourself
2. Know your mentee
3. Gather complete information related to your mentee
4. Schedule mentoring meetings frequently
5. Establish strong bonding and relationship
6. Be professional and give complete information
7. Spend time
8. Select suitable place for conduction of meeting
9. Record the important issues and maintain the confidentiality
10. Check the progress periodically and give feedback

3.5 Outcomes of Mentoring

1. Positive outlook
2. Discipline
3. Strong value system
4. Obedience
5. Respect
6. Thankfulness
7. Gratitude
8. Ethics
9. Responsibility and accountability
10. Value for time and resources
11. Self-reputation
12. Helpful
13. Strong minded
14. Explore his/her talents
15. Good citizens

3.6 Benefits to Mentors

If the above tips are implemented and considered ethically

and seriously by all teachers then I am sure this process will bring JOY and SATISFACTION that no reward or recognition can bring in. We are answerable to our own conscience. Let us remember that and be more responsible in what we do. Mentoring can happen at all levels, so it is clear mentoring is needed for all and at all levels. Let us join hands in making this process more effective and result oriented. If this world has to be a better place then we need to be better individuals, let's correct and mould ourselves to be better citizens and let's find the purpose of our life.

3.7 Health and Hygiene: Physical and Mental Activity

During the pandemic it is important that all faculties take care of their health first and avoid social interactions. All communication made to faculty emphasised on how every faculty should take care of the physical and mental health. While at the campus, the Physical Director ensured that breathing techniques and exercise sessions were conducted maintaining social distancing.

Even during the lock down faculty were constantly reminded of indulging in physical exercise. It was made clear to all faculties that their weight would be checked as soon as they enter the campus and this was followed in principle. Faculty were encouraged to take the staircase rather than use the lifts in order to ensure that it became a part of their routine and helped in physical fitness. For mental health a session by Swami Sukhabhodhananda was organised on a virtual platform.

The below guidelines will help in building physical fitness and mental health for all employees and that which also includes faculty who work from home and students who are taking up online classes:

1. It is mandatory for all employees and students of REVA to build their immunity. Proper nutrition and diet intake is a must.

Online Course On
6 Hidden Secrets Of Mantra Healing
On June 6th Saturday
11:00 AM To 12:00 PM

2. Cut down on unnecessary time spent on social media. Instead form good habits of meditation and regular physical exercises.
3. During lock down period and also while spending more time at home, maintain your regular schedule of waking up, going to bed, eating timings as usual.
4. Form a good hobby, if you don't have one, now and practice that every day. It can be cooking, reading, maintaining a diary, learning a new skill, etc. which will keep your mind occupied.
5. It is important to stay positive. Don't ignore your mental health. If you suddenly feel depressed, anxious, fatigued, tired, angry, worried, etc. very frequently, don't hesitate to talk to your mentors, teachers, family and friends. If required, take help of psychological counsellors.
6. News intake: The constant observation and watching of news in TV affect the mental health of individuals and concentrate on book reading and involve in household works and gardening etc.
7. Routine works: Most of the students who come from hostels have different routine and they need to adjust with the family. They need to change their routine by involving with family. Try to have lunch and dinner with all the members.
8. Exercise: It is important to engage in work during free time like walking, workouts in the open area etc. to keep fit.
9. Enjoy your work: Some of the activities listening music, podcasts, making art, watch movies, and more to be done and try to engage in one activity each day that brings joy.
10. Blood test and weight check is mandatory for all staff members and wearing of masks is must.
11. Give importance to Ayurveda in developing immunity through the regular practice of drinking warm water throughout the day, practicing yoga and meditation, use of turmeric, coriander, and garlic in cooking.

12. Educate importance of *tulsi* leaves. Suggested that 2-3 leaves can be put into the water dispensing unit.
13. Impart the knowledge on the importance of Health Insurance to all sections of society as poor are less aware of the insurance schemes.
14. Providing an agile digital healthcare infrastructure to accommodate dynamically changing scenarios.
15. Stress management and related subjects to be a part of online classes.
16. Eating healthy meals and keeping up with personal hygiene is important.
17. Ensuring that fear is not passed on or experienced is considered a state of mind and is to be followed.

3.8 Campus Readiness

Our campus is safe and set and ready for our students if the Government asks to open the campus. The following measures have all been taken up and put in place for safety of employees and students.

REOPENING THE GATES OF
REVA POST LOCKDOWN
REVA
UNIVERSITY
June 2020

REVA UNIVERSITY
Overview
At REVA, we are committed to putting our people first. With COVID-19 officially listed as a pandemic by the World Health Organization (WHO), and with so much yet to understand, we wanted to take a moment to let you know the extraordinary and proactive steps we are taking to ensure your safety.
We have implemented a number of guidelines that will help us reduce exposure to and transmission of a range of illnesses, including the Novel Coronavirus. Do read through this document and gain essential information on the measures taken by us to reopen the University in a safe manner.

REVA UNIVERSITY
A friendly Reminder
Wear a mask at all times
Wash your hands regularly
Maintain social distancing
Refrain from touching your face
Practice proper coughing & sneezing etiquettes
Avoid crowded events

Precautions taken by REVA

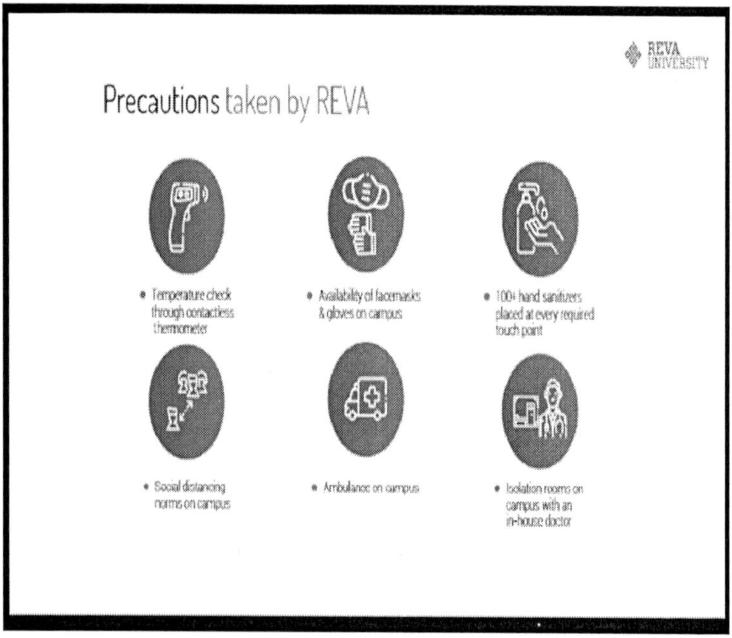
REVA UNIVERSITY
Precautions taken by REVA
Temperature check through contactless thermometer
Availability of facemasks & gloves on campus
100+ hand sanitizers placed at every required touch point
Social distancing norms on campus
Ambulance on campus
Isolation rooms on campus with an in-house doctor

Hygiene Surroundings

- Spitting inside the campus is strictly prohibited
- As per the Govt. order, spitting is a punishable offence and will be fined
- Trash should be disposed in the garbage bins only

Guidelines for

- Faculty and Employees
- Students
- Hostel Students
- Vendors and Shopkeepers

Accordingly maps have been prepared to be shared with faculty and students digitally.

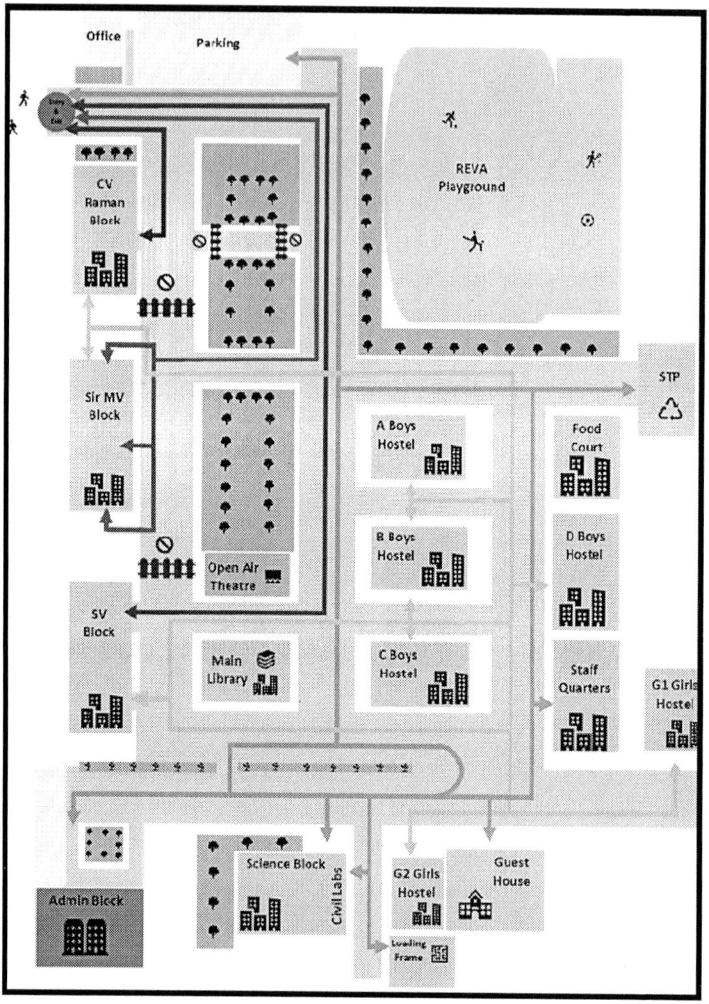

Walkway Map

Map/Directions for Students' Movement in Corridors

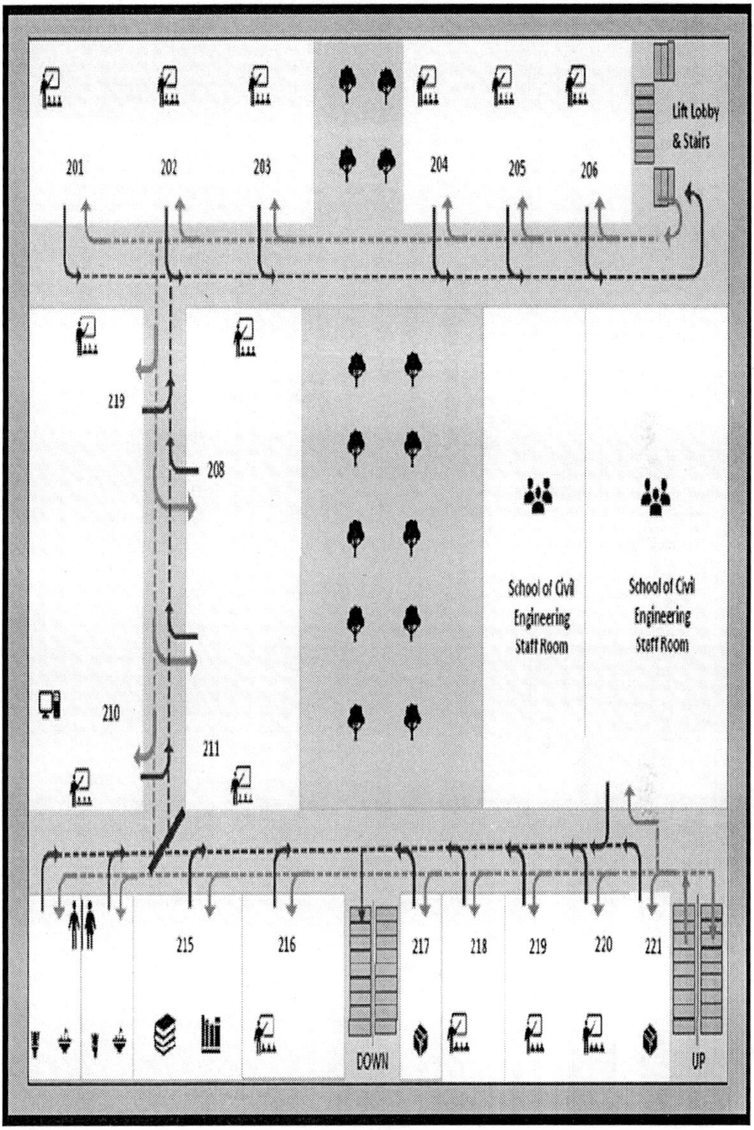

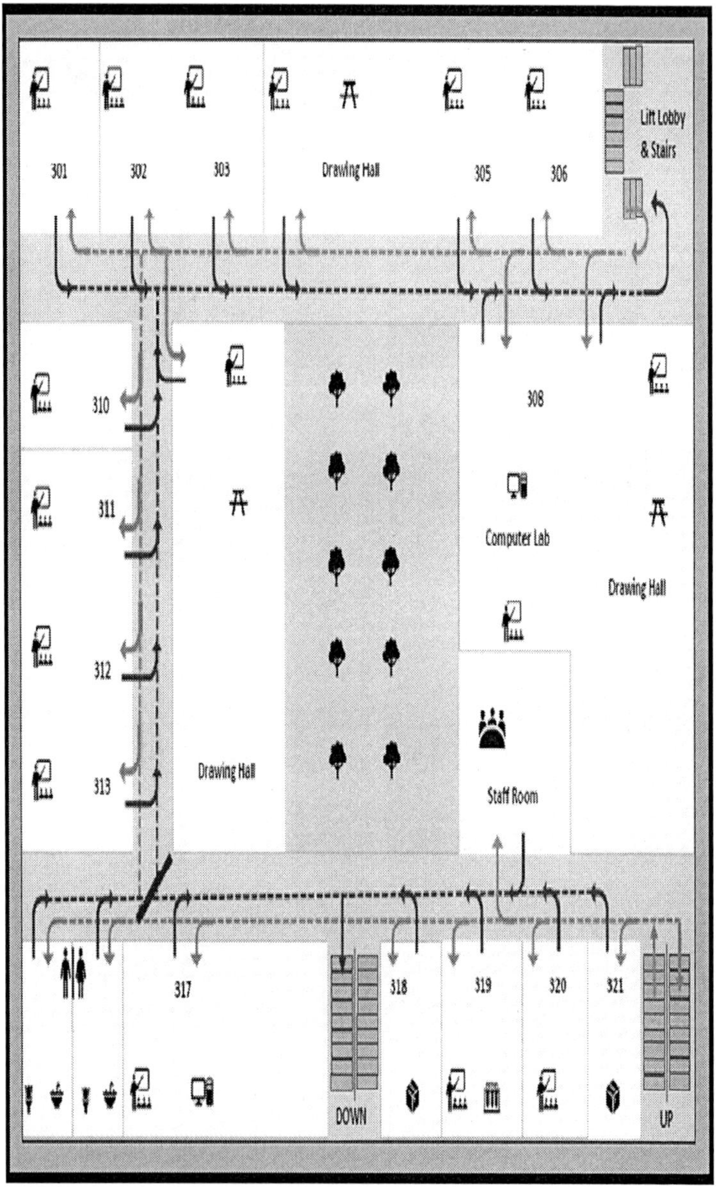

301
302
303
Drawing Hall
305
306
Lift Lobby & Stairs
310
311
312
313
Drawing Hall
308
Computer Lab
Drawing Hall
Staff Room
317
DOWN
318
319
320
321
UP

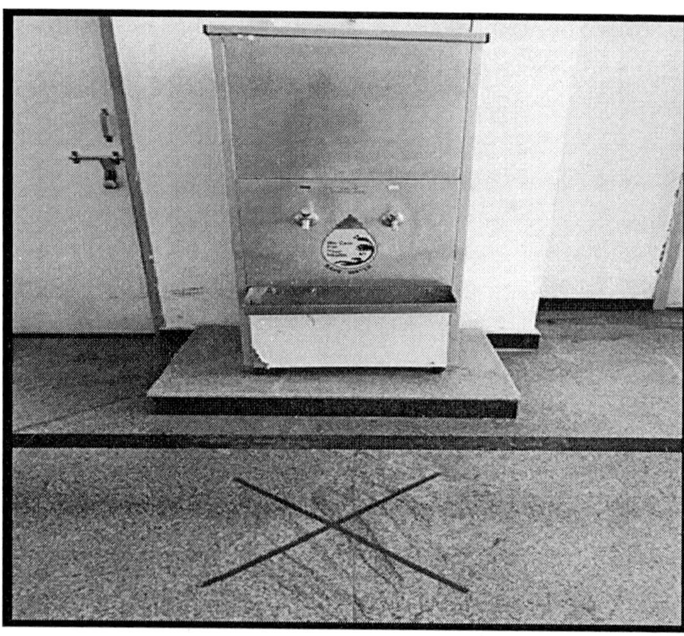

Typical Class Room Seating Plan 50% Capacity

Typical Classroom Layout (proposed) – Sl. No. 1 to 36

NOTE: Students shall be seated on first-come-first basis as per numbered sequence

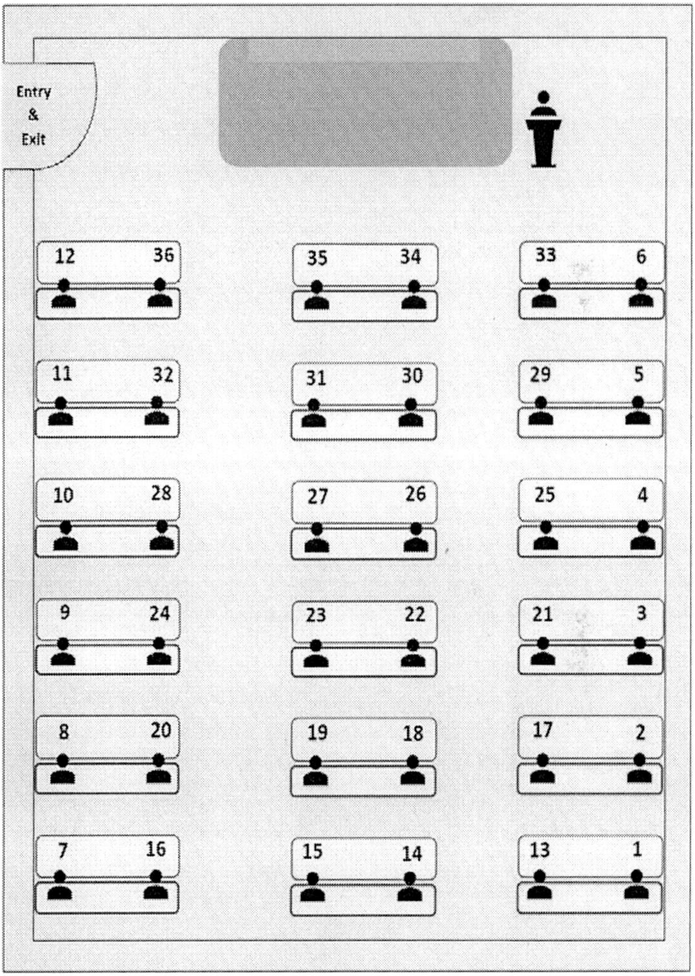

Typical Classroom Layout (proposed) – Sl. No. 37 to 72

NOTE: Students shall be seated on first-come-first basis as per numbered sequence

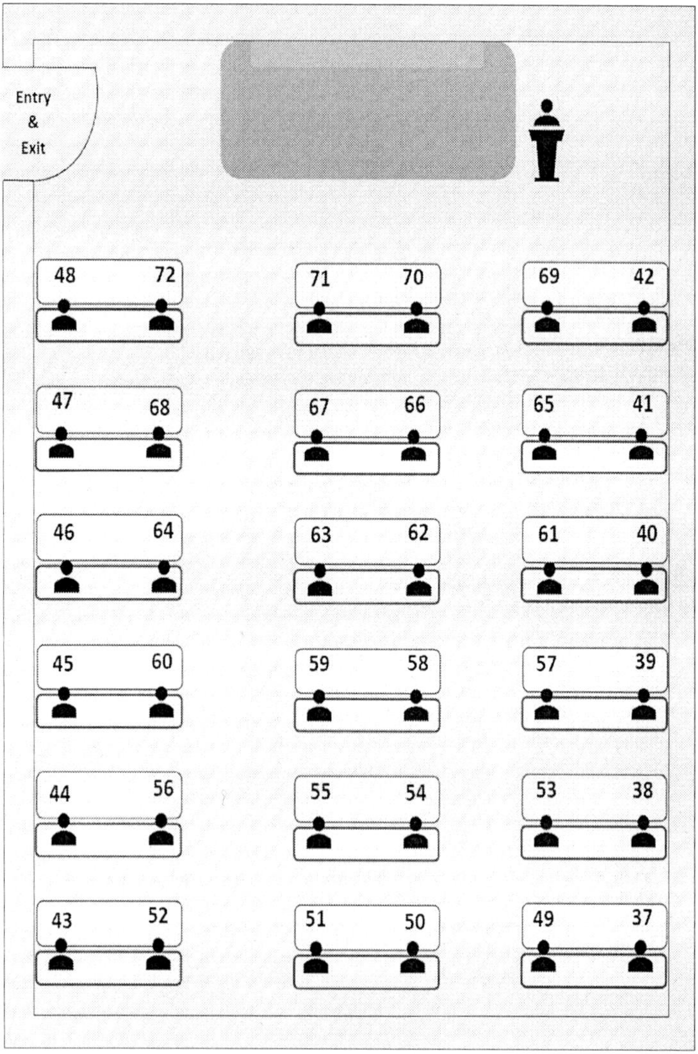

3.9 Digital Readiness

REVA has always been a front runner in implementing new technology. Accordingly new initiatives during this lock down to meet industry best practices in delivering quality education using technology framework and IT infrastructure services has been taken up.

3.9.1 IT Infrastructure: REVA has built-up a strong technology eco system and support team to meet student and user requirements. To ensure great user experience with seamless support, the IT Infrastructure services has been designed as per industry best practices and ITIL framework to ensure every user gets required support as per SLA defined. This will ensure best delivery, support and operation model to reach student, faculties and other users in the Campus.

3.9.2 Culture and Eco-system: Every student is unique and we want their learning with REVA also to be unique. We at REVA created an eco-system to ensure each student get an industry experience, during the learning process. REVA integrated all applications and services accessible with REVA official email ID. Students can now access all services across the campus using their email ID and password supplied by Department of IT.

3.9.3 Project Management: Multiple teams of professors and students have been created to work on development projects using Project Management practices with Agile and Waterfall methodology. Working on live project using Project Management methodology will make them ready and quick placement as soon as they complete their learning at REVA.

Resilient, redundant and scalable environment has been created for seamless learning experience. Every bit of access to e-content, online lectures deliveries, submission of assignments and appearing for the Semester end Exams were fully secured to ensure zero infringement. We at REVA have given equal importance to student safety, continuous learning and upskilling with latest technologies with the help of certification programs in association with Coursera.

We analysed there are 3 important factors in online education delivery i.e. e-content, collaboration and communication. We at REVA created small teams at departmental level to create best e-learning content to meet student and industry expectations. The e-content library would cover all required program, subjects and topics with crisp, focussed and engaging content. It would be more project and concept based learning, including impressive power point presentations powered by the best mentors, training to the students seating across the network, best video lectures which includes interactive discussion and cross communication using platform like Microsoft Teams.

To keep sanity of the content, we have ensured that each content is created by a team of faculties, verified by the subject matter experts and quality tested by the department heads. The Department of IT will make sure that each lecture delivery needs to be seamless with great user experience. Required training and SOP has been shared with each user group to ensure due support can be provided in case of any incident reported.

To keep data and personal security, REVA has implemented ISMS-27001 policies on their network along with data encryption. Which ensures every bit of data transported with in campus network and send outside network is end to end protected. The Content with user information shared during the classes or any communication is secured.

3.10 E-Content

Curriculum is influenced by content and pedagogy, but very often there has been lot of apprehensions about the content delivered and pedagogy adopted. Curriculum should focus on meeting the requirements of Students, Teachers and Industry. Developing e-content was entirely a new process for faculty members. This needs lot of training and guidelines that needs to be given to faculty members. Bringing change is important but hand holding our faculty in this process of change is equally important and giving them clarity on the same will enable them to prepare the e-content as per the standards expected.

In the process of developing the e-content it is important that you should first have proper clarity about the course that you are expected to deliver. Firstly read the course structure, course type, course objectives, course outcomes, curriculum pertaining to the course in detail to have a better clarity and understanding of the course. Make sure that you have complete knowledge about what exists in each and every unit of the course. Also study the credit pattern and the time duration in which the course needs to be delivered. Since at REVA University we follow outcome-based education, mapping the outcomes with the programs outcomes is essential. Through this by the end of the course you will be able to understand the course attainment percentage and the attainment percentage of the program outcomes.

For teaching each course, knowledge and adopting the appropriate course pedagogy is important. Depending on the nature and type of the course decide appropriate pedagogy to be adopted. The purpose and objective of delivering a course should not only be that all students pass in the respective course, but the focus should be on attainment of delivered outcomes through the courses.

The e-content should focus on the current and also throw light on the future scenario and the content so developed should be relevant. While preparing the e-content technical specification should also be taken care like following a proper branded template of the University, proper logical sequential flow line has to be ensured while preparing the e-content. Proper and uniform font style, font size needs to be followed in your PPT's.

Do not overload your presentations with too much of information. As far as possible be precise, specific and to the point. Use of images, animated pictures, diagrams, graphs, charts, videos could form a part your e-content to make the content impressive and attractive from learner of view. E-content authoring should be done with ethical academic standards, use proper referencing, citations, links and wherever applicable give credit to the original author. Do not replicate, copy or duplicate instead reflect your thoughts.

The e-content development process should be a well-planned activity with a preparation schedule in place. Verification of e-content should happen at three levels of the School level. Two levels of verification by team leads and then by Assistant Director and School Director, One external random review is also necessary to be done by an external. To know the originality of the content so developed it is also advisable to go for plagiarism check. Prepare the assignments, quizzes and assessment questions pertaining to your courses. E-content and course handouts should match with one another. E-content developed should also give information regarding reference books to be referred and suggested readings for each unit, so that the student attends the classes with preparations. E-content should also cater to the practical component i.e. laboratory related courses where videos pertaining to laboratory experiment is to be recorded. Communication and language part to be kept in mind and dress code also to be professional too. Studio recording could also be done on the basis of e-content developed.

For e-content to be developed 4 quadrants has to be focused upon:

I Quadrant: Content Development	**II Quadrant:** Preparation from Faculty
III Quadrant: Quality of the Content	**IV Quadrant:** Technical Specifications

3.11 Placement Readiness and Virtual Placement

During this COVID-19 pandemic situation, REVA University Career Development Centre has come out with online training and virtual hiring process. We are trying to find and establish a new equilibrium and a new normal in career development. Face 360 training of 64 hrs is on process for engineering schools and MCA students which will help the students to get ready for the recruitment. Virtual hiring process has been initiated both from the company and also from the University. In this regard, video conference has been conducted between REVA University and Mindtree, Capgemini, Zenken, Wipro, DXC Technologies, TCS, Endurance, Eurofins, AMD, SAP Labs, and HPE.

We have already taken online registration for recruitment process through our Bizotic app and also initiated video resume of all registered students to be submitted in to the app. Virtual recruitment process for the outgoing batch 2021 will commence from mid of July 2020 onwards. The companies who have agreed to participate are Mindtree, Capgemini, DXC Technologies, TATA Elxsi, Endurance, Eurofins, AMD, HPE, Publicis Sapient, Global Logic & TCS Codevita.

The CDC will ensure that, the pandemic will not affect the work culture and continue to put effort for better placements and career.

Career Development Centre at REVA University is all set for Virtual recruitment process and all training in this regard is given to the batch that would face the interviews remotely in the year 2021. After successfully placing all our passing out and eligible graduates of 2020 batch, the CDC is now all set to take up the process for the passing out batch 2021.We at REVA always believe that students passing out of our University should not only walk out with the degree certificates but we most importantly believe in placing them in their dream companies.

This was one of the important reasons as to why we completed the examinations online for our students' especially final semester to ensure that they do not miss the job offers that they already had in hand. Today even in this prevailing situation of COVID-19 our students have joined the companies and they have also started working and I am happy to hear from them that they have already received their first month salary too.

During the uncertain times our students are still certain about the efforts put in by our Career Development Centre, who have already started the process for the graduating students of 2021 batch. We always believe in giving our best to the stakeholders, whatever may be the situation we do not want our stakeholders to miss out on anything, our stakeholders are our first priority and their interest is always our concern.

Parents always dream about their ward's future be it academics or their career, in this regard we are always with them in giving them a direction and hope about their career. The CDC at REVA University has THREE wings, first wing concentrates on training and grooming students both in soft skills and technical aspects through the well trained trainers. Second wing focuses on the process of recruitment and the third wing encourages interested students to take up competitive examination for civil services by professionally training them.

Virtual recruitment is nothing but hiring remotely without having an interaction with the candidate directly but instead the recruiters remotely host video interviews to evaluate the applicants remotely. In this situation of uncertainty and when there is concern for health and safety today hiring, training and on boarding of candidates is happening remotely. In this regard it is important for us to prepare the graduating students for all the challenges and uncertainties that the future holds for them and also make them competent and confident in all situations.

3.11.1 Recruitment Migration from Taboo Process to Virtual: Company's response to stimuli for global pandemic was agile knitting of virtual paradigm. Days of persuasion has gone by, it's time to marvel the recruiters with your talents. Following the unforeseen disruption of the corona virus pandemic, hiring companies are now resorting to intelligent automated systems that offer virtual screening environment and interviewing experience, instead of conducting in-person interviews. Survey Report found that 98.9 percent of employers recruit from traditional empanelled Universities. REVA has its array of 250+ recruiters who hire talents annually.

In today's dynamic world, talent is the riding force for business and skills are the driving force for talent. These recruiters have shifted gears from an orthodox hiring to niche hiring of talents based on hackathons and coding skills which contributes to real life scenarios and business challenges. Recruiters are indulging their recruits in fellowship programs to make them involved and also motivate them to strive well to achieve peaks in their respective careers.

The corrosive gap between the pandemic and the deterioration of jobs in the market is the launch pad that has to be used by fresh graduates to plunge and cling to their career path.

3.11.2 What is Virtual Campus Recruiting?

Virtual interview and its working

Virtual interview is a process where the recruiter will get connected with an aspiring job seeker remotely through a common platform of interaction. This will be an AV interaction. The recruiter also will get an insight of the candidate through digital resume.

Technology used in Virtual Hiring

Pre-hiring assessments from the established portals will be conducted for initial screening. Recruiters leverage on online platforms, virtual chat room and video conferencing for hosting the full recruitment cycle. Few companies precede the use of Artificial Intelligence to scale talent based on parameters of speed, precision and also soft skills.

The Preparation Required for Virtual Recruitment

Preparation plays a vital role in virtual recruitment. The 3 Ts for excelling in Virtual Interview include:

(a) Technology

Technology is gaining prominence as more job roles require digital competencies. Test your gadgets, operational fluency and its connectivity before an interview.

(b) Tumult less: choose a space with less distraction, noise and proper lighting

(c) Tranquillity: being calm and composed brings the best out of you

Preparing students for the Virtual Hiring Process

1. Test Your Technology: The minute a graduate is invited for a virtual interview, s/he has to test his/her knowledge of technology to ensure that the graduate is competent enough to handle the technology successfully. Check of internet connectivity and confirming the camera and microphone are working comes second. The graduate needs to buy a mini webcam with a built-in microphone and ensure everything is set up 15 minutes before the interview commences and be ready. If the picture is grainy or the graduate experiences an echo they should not panic at the last moment. Care is to be taken to check on audio or lighting during the call.

2. Set the Scene and Minimize Distractions: While testing technology, graduate must determine where to take the interview. They need to find a room with optimal lighting, preferably near a window, or a blank wall to guarantee that the graduate is the focal point of the conversation. Clean up of r surroundings is a must. It is hard to convince the employer that the graduate is planned and organized when there is laundry visibly piling up in the corner of the room. Once settled, care to be taken to eliminate all distractions. Turning off the TV, silencing the cell phone and closing all windows to muffle neighbourhood traffic is a must.

3. Sitting Down with Preparedness: Just because the graduate is on a computer it does not mean that s/he can search the web for answers during the process of interview, so avoiding browsing is a must. The graduate should appear focused and ready to answer any questions without the help of the internet. Research about the company before appearing for the interview and jotting down notes for easy reference has to be done. It is also best to come prepared with answers to most frequently asked interview questions such as:

- Why are you interested in this role?
- What do you know about our company?
- What is your biggest weakness?
- What are your short-term goals and long-term goals?
- What are your strengths and hobbies?
- Talk about your project/internship you have done in the course of your graduation.

Memorizing each response should be avoided. Instead, writing some high-level thoughts down on post-its and sticking them to the computer can be done.

4. Practice, Don't Memorize: Training graduates not to sound robotic throughout the interview, whether answering or asking questions, or giving an elevator pitch has to be done. It is a good idea to run through a few practice rounds with a friend or family member. This will give the graduate a chance to rehearse with different personalities and answer a variety of different questions. While it may be awkward, rehearsing has a safe atmosphere to make mistakes and learn from them, so that the graduate is better prepared for the actual scenario. It is important to keep things simple. One should be made aware not to give a long-winded answer if the question does not require it. Being clear and concise is one of the most important things in a job interview.

5. Monitoring Body Language: One cannot firmly shake a hiring manager's hand or as easily exude enthusiasm via video. But what one can do is monitor body language.

The main way to communicate confidence is to sit up straight, smile, and keep the camera at eye level. Research shows that employers are more likely to remember what the graduate said when one maintains eye contact, so focus on the camera when talking and not on the image of the hiring manager is a must.

6. Dress: Dressing as one would for an in-person interview is a must. For boys, that might mean a button-up shirt, blazer, and formal clothes, while girls can consider western formals or traditional formal dress code Professional clothing will show you are serious about the position, but there are personal benefits as well: Studies show that people feel "most authoritative, trustworthy, and competent when wearing formal business attire."

7. Establish a Connection: One never knows how many interviews a company may conduct for a position. One might be at the end of a long list of people the hiring manager spoke to that day. This is why it is important to make a connection. Graduates must not be afraid to have a short aside about a common interest. The recruiter might enjoy the break from the routine questions they have to get through.

8. Being Oneself: A key task for a recruiter is determining whether the graduate would be a good fit for the company's culture. This can be challenging during a virtual interview because there is a physical disconnect. It is more difficult for the interviewer to understand enthusiasm through the screen, so making sure that the graduate is expressive when answering questions is a must.

9. Introspection & Feedback: Once the interview is completed, graduates must make it a practice to share feedback to the school coordinator and also to CDC.

Guidelines that can be shared with a candidate:

1. Once you register for the drive, it is mandatory to participate.
2. Please wear the University Id card during interview/test time.
3. Please do not request for postponement/rescheduling of the test.
4. Timings of the test to be adhered to.
5. Check the internet connectivity and power back up.

6. You must be aware that the online test/interviews will be proctored.
7. Multiple usage of devices/portals during online test is viewed very seriously and will invite disqualification of the candidature. The student will not be allowed for any other further drives conducted by CDC.
8. The system (laptop/desktop) should be updated with the recent version of software for usage.
9. Keep your resume ready with photograph & necessary documents (soft and hard copy).

3.11.3 Training Offered through CDC

The training activity for the passing out batch 2021 has already commenced and all graduating students are expected to register themselves with the Career Development center using BIZOTIC app. The companies have accepted to hire students virtually during this pandemic situation and most of the companies are likely to start their process shortly.

Students apart from all this were given online training for employability through employability courses from reputed MOOCs platforms too. Students are also trained to upload their video resume in BIZOTIC app and upload all their grade cards and add on certificates using the app. Students need to be well equipped with this entire new process and should know how they can effectively communicate and present their credentials to the recruiter.

In this entire process we support and strengthen our students with all that is required to ensure that they ultimately reach their goals. University always assures the competent and eligible students with job offers of their choice and nevertheless students who are not interested in being employed are mentored to take up self-employment by nurturing their entrepreneurial skills for which REVA Nest our incubation center provides all facilities and support for budding entrepreneurs.

Students with entrepreneurial zeal and mindset are allowed to present their innovative ideas with clarity on business plan and feasibility report, assistance is provided to promote entrepreneurship which can create jobs in the future for many others. As a University, we would like to produce graduates who are serious in setting up enterprise of their own, in this regard we do offer programs on new venture planning and Family business management which is opening up lot of opportunities to young talented students'. This is in a way a small contribution of the University towards nation building.

3.12 Central Library Readiness

Within the library seating arrangements have been made maintaining social distance when students return to campus. All the book racks will be sanitized frequently when students are there in campus. Accordingly all study tables will be sanitized on a regular basis. Traffic flow walkways are done for social distancing. Self E-gate login system is arranged by avoiding manual entries. Self-book issue with the help of kiosk machine and self-book return with the help of book drop machine is in place. Student can access library e-resources like e-journals, e-books, e-question papers etc., where ever they are. Through remote access all users can access library e-resources like e-journals, e-books, e-question paper etc., from their residences also.

3.13 REVA NEST

During the pandemic era we will strive to accommodate incubates shift to remote work operations. We aim to explore the critical competencies to collaborate digitally, and be prepared to adjust incubate experience strategies. During this time REVA will provide support by considering personal factors rather than external factors taking precedence over what matters for incubates. Employing such measures can be an effective way to promote physical health and improve the emotional well-being. We will also build a more responsive organization, design roles and structures around outcomes to increase agility and flexibility and formalize how processes can flex. Employees will be provided with varied, adaptive and flexible roles so that they acquire cross-functional knowledge and training.

While at the campus, adapting to the new normal with best practices we shall ensure that safely distanced workstations are set. Co-working spaces will undergo frequent sanitization checks and the highest precautionary measures will be followed by the hour every single day. We shall go ahead and optimize the space and avoid community meetings. Virtual Mentoring will be the preferred mode for interactions. As a part of the process safety manuals to members physically and electronically will be given. All members will be encouraged to use messengers, video calls and e-mail correspondence instead of business meetings.

3.14 Virtual Farewell

For the first time perhaps in the country, REVA University organized the first ever virtual farewell programme. Every single student moving out of the university campus after studying for 3 to 4 to 5 years will always dream of having a farewell programme for themselves. Due to COVID and the disruptions created by it, students have been sad that they could not even say goodbye to each other face to face. As is customary this time of the year is when students are also given their awards and certificates for all their proficiency. Sadly, some of them have given up hopes on that recognition that every university gives. But then here are some universities who have gone ahead and ensured that none of their students miss out on those golden moments and memories. One such university which has been ensuring that students of the graduating batches of REVA do not feel that they did not get a proper farewell from the University has been REVA University, Bangalore. With the disruptions in life caused by the pandemic, the University has been brilliantly combating against all odds as the University was in time to support the academic support required for students and remote instruction was extended to all students. This being completed, the University spared no efforts to ensure that the students were administered their semester end exams in time and in an online mode and with all challenges faced in a planned manner. Thereafter, remained the farewell programme for the outgoing students of the year 2020. REVA University went ahead and planned this programme meticulously at the Kuvempu Auditorium of REVA University where the outgoing batch of students of REVA were given an online farewell. Some glimpses of the coverage made.

Newspapers

Prajavani

ಎಂಜಿನಿಯರಿಂಗ್ ವಿದ್ಯಾರ್ಥಿಗಳಿಗೆ ಆನ್‌ಲೈನ್‌ನಲ್ಲೇ ಬೀಳ್ಕೊಡುಗೆ

ಬೆಂಗಳೂರು: ರೇವಾ ವಿಶ್ವವಿದ್ಯಾಲಯದ ಅಂತಿಮ ಸೆಮಿಸ್ಟರ್‌ನ ಎಂಜಿನಿಯರಿಂಗ್ ವಿದ್ಯಾರ್ಥಿಗಳಿಗೆ ಆನ್‌ಲೈನ್‌ನಲ್ಲಿಯೇ ಬೀಳ್ಕೊಡಲಾಯಿತು.

ಕಾರ್ಯಕ್ರಮ ಉದ್ಘಾಟಿಸಿ ಮಾತನಾಡಿದ ವಿಶ್ವವಿದ್ಯಾಲಯದ ಕುಲಪತಿ ಡಾ.ಪಿ. ಶ್ಯಾಮರಾಜು, 'ಲಾಕ್‌ಡೌನ್ ಕಾರಣದಿಂದ ವಿದ್ಯಾರ್ಥಿಗಳಿಗೆ ಬೀಳ್ಕೊಡುಗೆ ಕಾರ್ಯಕ್ರಮ ತಪ್ಪಬಾರದು ಎಂಬ ಉದ್ದೇಶದಿಂದ ಆನ್‌ಲೈನ್‌ನಲ್ಲಿಯೇ ಈ ಕಾರ್ಯಕ್ರಮ ಆಯೋಜಿಸಲಾಗಿದೆ. ಇದಕ್ಕಾಗಿ ಐಟಿ ಸಿಬ್ಬಂದಿ ಹಗಲಿರುಳು ಶ್ರಮಿಸಿದ್ದಾರೆ' ಎಂದರು.

'ಅಂತಿಮ ವರ್ಷದ ವಿದ್ಯಾರ್ಥಿಗಳಿಗೆ ಭವಿಷ್ಯದ ಬಗ್ಗೆ ಅನೇಕ ಕನಸುಗಳಿರುತ್ತವೆ. ಅದಕ್ಕೆ ಧಕ್ಕೆಯಾಗಬಾರದು ಎಂಬ ಕಾರಣಕ್ಕೆ ಆನ್‌ಲೈನ್‌ನಲ್ಲಿಯೇ ಪರೀಕ್ಷೆ ನಡೆಸಿ, ಫಲಿತಾಂಶ ನೀಡಲಾಗಿದೆ' ಎಂದರು.

Deccan Herald

REVA University holds virtual farewell

BENGALURU, DHNS: City-based REVA University recently held a virtual farewell for its final year engineering students.

Inaugurating the virtual farewell, university chancellor Dr P Shyama Raju lauded the efforts of the varsity staff in organising the programme, hailing them as "Reva Warriors".

Addressing the students, Dr Raju said: "The future of the students is more important to me than my own life. Ever since the lockdown, I have been visiting the campus daily and holding over 10 meetings. I had also interacted with the students and parents to understand their problems."

Reaffirming his commitment to brighten the higher education and career prospects of the students, Dr Raju said the varsity held exams online and delivered the results. "Today, we are happy that we achieved what had been promised to the students."

All the students of the final semester engineering courses participated in the virtual farewell.

Kannada Prabha

ವಿದ್ಯಾರ್ಥಿಗಳಿಗೆ ಆನ್‌ಲೈನ್‌ನಲ್ಲೇ ಸೆಂಡ್‌ಆಫ್!

ಕೊರೋನಾ ಎಫೆಕ್ಟ್: ದೇಶದಲ್ಲೇ ಮೊದಲ ಬಾರಿ ರೇವಾ ವಿವಿ ವಿನೂತನ ಪ್ರಯತ್ನ | ಪೋಷಕರ ಮೆಚ್ಚುಗೆ

ಅಂದು ಇಂಜಿನಿಯರಿಂಗ್ ವಿದ್ಯಾರ್ಥಿಗಳ ಬೀಳ್ಕೊಡುಗೆ ಸಮಾರಂಭ

ಕನ್ನಡಪ್ರಭ Thu, 25 June 2020
https://kpepaper.asianetnews.com/c/52988004

Andhra Jyothi

విద్యార్థుల భవిష్యత్తే ముఖ్యం

- దేశంలోనే తొలి ఆన్‌లైన్ ఫేర్‌వెల్ కార్యక్రమం - రేవా యూనివర్సిటీ చాన్స్‌లర్ డాక్టర్ పీ శ్యామరాజు

బెంగళూరు, జూన్ 26 (ఆంధ్రజ్యోతి): కొవిడ్-19 పెను సవాల్ విసిరిందని, దీని నుంచి మనమంతా సాధ్యమైనంత త్వరగా బయటపడి మళ్లీ సాధారణ జీవితం గడుపుదామని రేవా యూనివర్సిటీ చాన్స్‌లర్ డాక్టర్ పీ శ్యామరాజు ఆకాంక్షను వ్యక్తం చేశారు. లాక్‌డౌన్ నేపథ్యంలో రేవా యూనివర్సిటీ ఫేర్‌వెల్‌ను ఆన్‌లైన్‌లో నిర్వహించారు. దేశంలో ఇదే తొలిసారిగా ఈ వినూత్న ప్రయత్నాన్ని నిర్వహించడం గమనార్హం. బుధవారం, గురువారం రెండు రోజుల పాటు క్యాంపస్‌లోని ఆడిటోరియంలో జరిగిన ప్రదాన కార్యక్రమాన్ని ఉద్దేశించి డాక్టర్ పీ శ్యామరాజు ప్రసంగించగా వేల సంఖ్యలో విద్యార్థులు తమ ఇళ్లల్లోనే కూర్చొని ఆయన ప్రసంగాన్ని ఆలకించారు. ఫేర్‌వెల్ కార్యక్రమాన్ని విజయవంతం చేశారు. తన ప్రాణం కంటే విద్యార్థుల భవిష్యత్తే ఎంతో ముఖ్యమని ఈ సందర్భంగా పీ శ్యామరాజు ఉద్వేగ భరితంగా పేర్కొన్నారు. ఫేర్‌వెల్ కార్యక్రమం ప్రతి విద్యార్థికి ఒక మధుర స్మృతి లాంటిదని, ప్రస్తుత కరోనా పరిస్థితుల నేపథ్యంలో ఈ కార్యక్రమాన్ని ఆన్‌లైన్‌లో నిర్వహించాల్సిన పరిస్థితి రావడం తనకు కూడా ఎంతో బాధగా ఉందన్నారు. లాక్‌డౌన్ ప్రకటించిన తక్షణం ఆన్‌లైన్ బోధనపై దృష్టి సారించి కోర్సులను, పరీక్షలను త్వరితగతిన పూర్తి చేశామని ఆయన వివరించారు. ఎంతో రిస్క్‌ను భరించి క్యాంపస్‌కు ప్రతిరోజూ వచ్చి పదికిపైగా సమావేశాలు నిర్వహించేవాడినన్నారు. విద్యార్థులు ఉజ్వల భవిష్యత్‌ను అందుకోవాలని ఆయన ఆకాంక్షించారు. క్యాంపస్‌ను వీడుతున్న సీనియర్లు జూనియర్ విద్యార్థులకు సదా మార్గదర్శకులు కావాలని, అలాగే అలుమిని అసోసియేషన్‌తో క్రియాశీలక పాత్ర పోషించాలని ఆయన పిలుపునిచ్చారు. ఫేర్‌వెల్‌లో భాగంగా ఆన్‌లైన్‌లో విద్యార్థులకు సర్టిఫికెట్లు ప్రదానం చేశారు. ఈ కార్యక్రమంలో రిజిస్ట్రార్ ఎం ధనుంజయ, డిపార్ట్‌మెంట్ డీన్‌లు పాల్గొన్నారు.

ఆన్‌లైన్ ఫేర్‌వెల్ కార్యక్రమాన్ని ప్రారంభిస్తున్న చాన్స్‌లర్ డాక్టర్ పీ శ్యామరాజు తదితరులు

ఆంధ్రజ్యోతి Sat, 27 June 2020
https://epaper.andhrajyothy.com/c/53041202

Vijaya Karnataka

ರೇವಾ ವಿವಿ ವಿದ್ಯಾರ್ಥಿಗಳಿಗೆ ವರ್ಚುವಲ್ ಫೇರ್‌ವೆಲ್

ಬೆಂಗಳೂರು: ಲಾಕ್‌ಡೌನ್ ಘೋಷಣೆಯಾದ ಬಳಿಕವೂ ಶೈಕ್ಷಣಿಕ ವರ್ಷಗಳು ಮೊಟಕಾಗಬಾರದು ಎಂಬ ಉದ್ದೇಶದಿಂದ ನಾನು ನನ್ನ ಜೀವನವನ್ನೂ ಲೆಕ್ಕಿಸದೇ ಪ್ರತಿ ನಿತ್ಯ ಕ್ಯಾಂಪಸ್‌ಗೆ ಬಂದಿದ್ದೇನೆ. ನಮಗೆ ನಮ್ಮ ಭವಿಷ್ಯಕ್ಕಿಂತ ವಿದ್ಯಾರ್ಥಿಗಳ ಭವಿಷ್ಯವೇ ಮುಖ್ಯ ಎಂದು ರೇವಾ ವಿಶ್ವವಿದ್ಯಾಲಯದ ಕುಲಾಧಿಪತಿ ಡಾ.ಪಿ.ಶ್ಯಾಮರಾಜು ಹೇಳಿದ್ದಾರೆ.

ಕೊರೊನಾ ಪರಿಸ್ಥಿತಿಯಿಂದಾಗಿ ರೇವಾ ವಿಶ್ವವಿದ್ಯಾಲಯ ಅಂತಿಮ ಸೆಮಿಸ್ಟರ್ ಎಂಜಿನಿಯರಿಂಗ್ ವಿದ್ಯಾರ್ಥಿಗಳಿಗೆ ಆಯೋಜಿಸಿದ್ದ 'ವರ್ಚುವಲ್ ಫೇರ್ ವೆಲ್'ನಲ್ಲಿ ಮಾತನಾಡಿದ ಅವರು, ''ಲಾಕ್‌ಡೌನ್‌ನಿಂದಾಗಿ ವಿದ್ಯಾರ್ಥಿಗಳಿಗೆ ಬೀಳ್ಕೊಡುಗೆ ಕಾರ್ಯಕ್ರಮ ತಪ್ಪಬಾರದೆಂದು ವರ್ಚುವಲ್‌ನಲ್ಲಿ ಆಯೋಜಿಸಿದ್ದೇವೆ,'' ಎಂದರು.

''ಉದ್ಯೋಗ ಮತ್ತು ಉನ್ನತ ಶಿಕ್ಷಣಕ್ಕೆ ಪ್ರವೇಶ ಪಡೆಯಲು ವಿದ್ಯಾರ್ಥಿಗಳು ಮುಂದಾಗುತ್ತಾರೆ. ಅವರ ಆಸೆಗಳು ಕಮರಬಾರದೆಂದು ನಾವು ಆನ್‌ಲೈನಲ್ಲಿಯೇ ಪರೀಕ್ಷೆ ನಡೆಸಿ ಫಲಿತಾಂಶ ನೀಡಿದ್ದೇವೆ. ಕೇಂದ್ರ ಸರಕಾರದ ಮಾರ್ಗಸೂಚಿ ಅನ್ವಯ ನಾವು ತರಗತಿ ಆರಂಭಿಸಲು ಸಿದ್ಧರಿದ್ದೇವೆ. ವಿದ್ಯಾರ್ಥಿಗಳಿಗೆ ಭಯ ಬೇಡ. ನಿಮ್ಮ ಮನೆಗಿಂತಲೂ ನಮ್ಮ ಕ್ಯಾಂಪಸ್ ಸುರಕ್ಷಿತವಾಗಿರುತ್ತದೆ ಎಂಬ ಭರವಸೆ ನೀಡುತ್ತೇನೆ,'' ಎಂದು ಡಾ.ಪಿ.ಶ್ಯಾಮರಾಜು ಹೇಳಿದರು.

TV Channels - Live

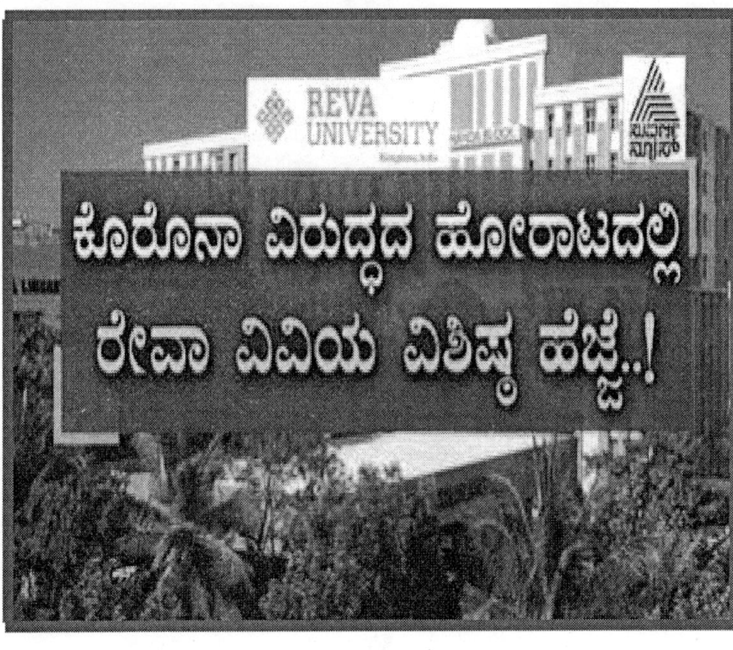

రేవా యూనివర్సిటీలో ఘనంగా ఆన్‌లైన్ ఫేర్‌వెల్ కార్యక్రమం
Fri, Jun 26
ABN
26:06:2020 22:25:46:23
COMING UP
గమ్మత్తు బాణీలకు కేరాఫ్ ఆర్డీ బర్మన్

ವಿವಿಯ ಚಾನ್ಸಲರ್ ಶ್ಯಾಮರಾಜು
ವಿದ್ಯಾರ್ಥಿಗಳಿಗೆ ಬೀಳ್ಕೊಡುಗೆ ಸಮಾರಂಭ
PUBLIC TV
ಬಿಡುಗಡೆಯಾದ ದಿನವೇ 'ರಾಮ್'ಬಾಣಕ್ಕೆ ಬ್ರೇಕ್..!?
ಏನು ಕಾರಣ..?
SBI Gold
LIVE

3.15 Concluding Notes

In this book I have only tried to summarize all my learnings and experience in implementing new thoughts and ideas during the unprecedented times. None of us were prepared for a situation like this, and education being ongoing it is very important that we bring in a paradigm shift in education. Teaching-learning has to go on, and youth have to continue their learning journey with the least hassles. The intention behind putting together my thoughts in the form of a book is to share the best practices of our University with readers. I am only hopeful that it would help some were along and be of use to those interested.

What Indian Education or the Educators across the globe are facing today is something that perhaps none of us have been witness to since the last World War. With lockdown being prompted time and again in various States in our country, educational institutions are rather uncertain about the commencement of the normal routine of the academic year. The longer term for education is a concern for all of us across the globe.

As educators we need to rethink and reimagine what will be the future of education to the Nextgen learners. While we were aware and cautious that technology based education was always the way forward for educators, that these disruptions would come this early and unprecedented is where the challenge lies. Time is now here for us to rethink how the future generation can be and what needs to be taught and what our students need to be prepared for. While grappling through these various scenarios that COVID has placed before us, there is a lot for us to learn from this pandemic.

Technology has to be a simple extension of an educator's profession. We need to replace the traditional structure with the modern technology requirement. COVID-19 has taught us how education needs to be changed and we need to be better prepared. The 21st century educator has seen a further change in his role. Students will now be able to gain better access to knowledge which they even otherwise were ahead of us. We need to now train our faculty to fit into a different role where they are no longer channels for communication of transfer of knowledge, but are thinkers and set students to think. Hence, their role is more of facilitators. Resilience and adaptability will be crucial for the next generations entering work.